First published in paperba
By Nev Mason Books (UK)

The right of Nev Mason to be identified as the author of this work has
been asserted by him in accordance with the copyright,
designs and patents act 1988.

A CIP catalogue record for this book is available from the British Library.

ISBN 978-1-910314-00-5

Typeset, printed and bound in Great Britain by;

www.direct-pod.com

www.nevmasonbooks.com

ACKNOWLEDGEMENTS TO:

JOHN DICKINSON AND TRIALS MOTOCROSS NEWS
DIRT BIKE RIDER MAGAZINE
M.C.N.
ALAN VOASE
DAVE JACKSON
DEREK LOCKWOOD

COVER DESIGN BY NEV MASON
WITH ALL THE ARTWORK
BY MICHAEL CASHMORE HINGLEY

THIS IS FOR MY LONG SUFFERING, DEVOTED
WIFE VAL, FOR NEARLY FIFTY YEARS OF A
VERY HAPPY MARRIAGE. SHE ENDURED
MANY HOURS OF ME IN MY OFFICE TYPING
THESE STORIES.
SO THANK YOU FOR YOUR PATIENCE, AND
FOR EDITING AND CORRECTING MY
SPELLING MISTAKES.

**NEV MASON, A VERY STRAIGHT TALKING
CHARACTER AS MOST PEOPLE FROM THAT PART
OF YORKSHIRE OFTEN ARE.**
QUOTE FROM M.C.N. JOURNALIST

Chapter 1

My first encounter with motorcycles, that I can remember, was when I was about three years old. Albert Mason, my father was a speedway rider and I was being pushed around the pits in my pram by Doris Mason my mother, and I can distinctly remember the deafening noise and the smell of the bikes. From that day on, I was hooked on motorcycles. Little did I know at that time, that throughout my entire life, I would encompass motorcycles in one form or another, both in the English and International motorcycle business world, and in motorcycle racing.

The war had finished and speedway was starting up again all over the UK and my parents took me and Pete, my older brother, to all the meetings that Dad rode at. Pete was three years older than me and had been riding motorcycles for about 2 years, and Dad had built him a special 150cc Triumph Terrier scrambles bike.

When I was about six, Dad decided to teach me to ride, on a James 125cc two stroke that he had bought for me. The first lesson was, and still is, vividly remembered by me. Sitting me on the petrol tank of the bike, he set off at a speed of about 5 miles an hour, then he jumped off the back, leaving me to try and keep the bike upright. I wasn't expecting this and the bike fell over into a ditch at the side of the lane, which was thick with nettles. I was trapped underneath the bike with the engine still madly revving away. I was rescued by Dad who stopped the engine and pulled the bike off me but I had nettle rash for days after this incident. My short pants and vest didn't give much protection from the nettles, but I really had enjoyed the five or six yards I'd managed to stay upright before the little James fell over on top of me.

About a week later I asked Dad if I could have another ride on the James, and this time he took me to a very large flat field for my lesson. He spent a few minutes, showing me how to work the throttle, brake and clutch, then we set off once again, with me sitting on the petrol tank. Again he jumped off the back of the bike and I was on my own. This time I was ready for it and made a conscious effort to hold the bike upright. I travelled across the field, to the far side, then I turned round in a big circle and wobbled back towards Dad. Growing in confidence and balance, I rode around for about half an hour before the bike finally ran out of

Me and Mam - Dad - Me and brother Pete

Dad's Ford Van

Matchless Scrambler - 14th birthday

Dot Scrambler - 12th birthday

petrol and came to a stop. Stationary, I was unable to hold the bike upright because my feet were six inches off the ground, so I jumped off sideways and rolled away from the bike as I hit the floor. This is something I have done many times throughout my life when racing in scrambles and moto cross. Pete was highly amused when I finally fell off, but disappointed it wasn't more dramatic. What I had managed to achieve on this second lesson was balance and confidence. Both are things anyone who learns to ride a bike knows about.

Dad put the James in the garage when we reached home and later, I spent two evenings with him, cutting and lowering the frame to reduce the seat height, so that I could reach the ground. I regularly used this little bike over the next few years, even learning how to use the hand change three speed gearbox, and clutch and brakes etc., and I remember enjoying many happy hours riding it.

Dad used to buy and sell second hand motorcycles for a living. As a boy he took me everywhere with him in his old blue, 30cwt Austin truck, which he used to collect and deliver them. We lived at Castle Bromwich, a few miles outside

Birmingham, though Mam and Dad were from East Yorkshire originally. Mam was from Skidby and Dad from Aldbourgh. He dealt in all makes of motorcycles and had a large number of both dealers, and non dealers that he regularly bought from, even travelling as far as Hull in Yorkshire. He specialized in competition motorcycles, speedway, trials, scrambles and road racing bikes, and his garage was always full of bikes.

Dad got side tracked for a couple of years helping to build the Lindley Test Track, MIRA near Nuneaton, where he ran a fleet of eighteen Ford and Bedford tipper trucks, carrying liquid concrete for building the banked test track. At nine years old, I drove one of the tipper trucks on this project.

Dad deemed it was not necessary for us kids to go to school, as both me and Pete were more use to him, driving his trucks on this large job, and even Mam drove a tipper truck. To me it was good fun driving these trucks, and I was getting paid, two pounds for a 7am to 6pm working day, six days a week, and I got free dinners. However all good things come to an end. The banked concrete track was eventually completely finished and he sold all his trucks and went back to buying and selling motorcycles again for a living.

This time he dealt in road bikes as well as competition bikes. He discovered that Ariel, Rudge and BSA road motorcycles could be bought plentifully and cheaply in Yorkshire. I remember, on one trip, he bought nine bikes and taking them to the Birmingham area, sold them for double what they were making in Yorkshire. He also found that Excelsior's, James and Francis Barnetts etc. were cheap to buy in the Midlands, and these he shipped to Yorkshire where they were a working man's dream.

I can never remember Dad having a cheque book, perhaps he did but I never saw any evidence of one, but he always carried about £1000 in cash with him. What I did notice was that he had a large circle of friends and business contacts who he dealt with. Dad was very good at making money but he was also very good at spending it, and so was Mam. I was with him at an auction when be bought a genuine ex Al Capone Hudson Terraplane, a big yank sports coupe, which he lost a week later in a bet.

When he needed quite large amounts of money for any of his business deals, there were about eight people, who must have trusted him implicitly, who he could go to. At a Kidderminster auction, I remember he had already bought two Aero Douglas 500cc, fore and aft, flat twins for himself, then lot 12, four brand new Gypsy Moth airplanes, still in their boxes came up. He bought all four planes for £10,000 which was a lot of money in those days. He borrowed the £10,000 from one of his money men and in less than a week he had sold all four planes to a guy in Australia for £18,000. He paid Jim, his lender £14000 back in cash and kept the remaining £4000 for himself. I was with him when he paid the guy his money back. Again the link was motor cycles, Jim owned a big house and grounds in Coleshill where he had a very large collection of road racing bikes which he bought, sold and sponsored people on.

In early 1953 my Grandma was taken ill and was taken to hospital in Hull. I recall driving through the night from the Midlands with Dad, to get to the hospital, but unfortunately she died half an hour before we arrived. In the past I had often been left with Grandma while Dad took bikes back to sell in Castle Bromwich. She was a strict disciplinarian and often gave me a sorting out if I cheeked her, but we had a strong bond and I had been very close to her. Things changed a lot after this. The house in Castle Bromwich was sold, but Dad kept the depot in Curdsworth he rented from Jim, and continued to buy and sell his bikes from here.

Now our home was in Hull, East Yorkshire. Dad rented a house and garage in Salmon Grove and made a couple of trips a week to Curdsworth to deliver bikes there and to pick up others for the return trip back to Hull. He now had a chap, based in Hull, who worked for him, fettling and tidying the bikes ready for sale. His name was Burt, I never did know his surname. Burt always dressed in a black, full length Navy greatcoat, he only ever ate Cadburys chocolate and all he ever drank was plain water. He was a brilliant mechanic but didn't look so good in the health stakes. He always had a deathly white complexion and only had five front teeth left. The chocolate had obviously taken its toll. He never ever wore socks and it didn't matter whether it was winter or summer, the only footwear he ever had was black wellies, but he was a really great person and very easy to get on with. He was a former grass track rider of some ability, and motorcycles were his true passion in life.

Burt hated women with a vengeance. Originally

from a well to do family in Pickering he felt he had been cheated out of his inheritance by his mother and two scheming sisters when his father died. All this had happened when he was 26 and he had spent the last 12 years travelling around England, living rough and doing casual mechanical work for motorcycle dealers to earn enough to keep him going. Now, aged 38 and not in the best of health he worked full time for Dad.

It was 1955 and I was aged 12, I didn't go to school, not very often anyway, just helped repair bikes and sell them in Dad's new motorcycle garage down West Dock Avenue, just off Hessle Road in Hull. Every Thursday afternoon Burt would take the 197 Dot scrambler Dad had bought for my 12th birthday, on the back of an ex army Austin pickup, to a scramble practice track at North Ferriby, or sometimes Melton. I remember spending hour after hour at these tracks, which led me to being able to go faster and faster over rough ground. Burt fussed around maintaining the bike and encouraging me from the side of the track to go faster into the corners. He also showed me how to go up and down hills fast and I crashed many times as I strove to go quicker and quicker.

Dad decided to rent a house and shop

approximately 100 yards from his motorcycle garage in West Dock Ave., so he could be nearer his business. We moved house from Salmon Grove, Cottingham Road, to our new home. This period of my life was good. I enjoyed going out every Thursday afternoon with Burt and practicing scrambling on my 197 Dot, but Dad and Mam would take both me and Pete, just about every Sunday, to Millington pastures near Pocklington, a typical Yorkshire Dales type area with large valleys and steep hills. At that time it was all totally unfenced and you could ride around it, unhindered, for miles. The family spent a lot of really good days there and one thing I can recall is that the place was infested with rabbits. Thousands of them living in warrens on the hill sides, but they were all wiped out by Myxomatosis. Within a year they were all gone and the place was never the same after they were all exterminated.

I had a major problem which became very apparent when I was left, for the first time, in charge of the shop one day, when Dad had gone out to collect some bikes he had bought. I was 13, and that day I sold a young guy who worked on the Trawlers as a deck hand, an ex GPO BSA Bantam for £14. 10s, a new

Corker helmet for £2.11.6d and a new back tyre for £2.2.6d. There would have been no problem if I had gone to school and learned to do sums, but I hadn't attended school for more than 18 months in my entire life, though until now it hadn't been a problem, or anything to worry about. I finally had to suffer the indignity of the 17 year old customer, who I was selling the bike and accessories to, having to add up the bill for me, as it became obvious to him I couldn't add it up myself. He paid the bill and luckily he was honest, and the amount was right when Dad checked it later. My next problem was when the lad asked for a bill of sale. The penny suddenly dropped; to do this job I would need to be able to read, write and do sums, and I couldn't do any of these things, it suddenly all clicked into place, that's what kids go to school for, to learn all these things.

At the back of the garage Burt had constructed a small living area for himself consisting of a wooden bunk bed built against the wall, plus a small table and a chair, with a radio which was always tuned into Radio Luxemburg. This was his home. Going to the back of the garage, Burt was working on a 600cc, ex works, Stan Banner Levis in the workshop. I asked him if he could make out a bill of sale for me as the customer was still out front waiting for one. He did this for me and I took the receipt out to the lad. Burt then asked me.

'Why didn't you write the receipt out for him?'

'Because I can't read or write, or do sums.' I answered

'So who added the bill up then?' he asked totally bewildered.

'The lad added them up for me.' I admitted. Burt who'd had a good education spent the next year, in between working on bikes, teaching me how to read and write. I did eventually learn to add up money by using my own, self taught method. Even now, aged 69, I still use my own way of working out maths, it works OK for me.

Throughout 1956 Dad's bike business had a steady growth. He was still buying bikes in Hull and taking them to his depot in Curdsworth, Midlands and bringing back small two stroke bikes to sell in his Hull garage. In November 1956, on my 14th birthday, I arrived at the garage and immediately noticed my Dot scrambler was not parked in its usual place. I asked Burt where it was .

'Your dad sold it yesterday to a guy from Beverley.'

'Why did he sell it?' I asked in an upset voice, Burt was now grinning broadly and he beckoned me to follow him into the workshop. On the middle bench was a bike with a cover over it, pulling the cover off the bike he burst into a loud chorus of,

'Happy birthday to you' and was joined by Mam, Dad and Pete who had all been hiding in the office. Sat on the bench was a gleaming 1955 Matchless 500 G80 CS scrambler, the same as my brother Pete's bike, only his bike was red and this one was black . These bikes were quite heavy but at 14 I weighed about 12 stone and was five feet nine inches tall.

'Do you want to go out on it this afternoon?' dad asked. Burt removed the bike from the work bench and now it was sitting on the floor, it looked massive to me. Climbing on, I couldn't believe how heavy it was compared to the Dot 197 I had been riding for the last two years. I did no work at all that morning, I just sat on the bike pretending I was riding it. Later that day I got to ride it for real at the Melton track . It was totally different from riding the Dot and it took me weeks to get used to it.

Dad's money man Jim, from Coleshill rang up that night and said there would be a large consignment of new 50cc scooters coming up for auction on Hull docks. They were, he had been told, destined to go to the States, but the importer had gone bust, so the scooters were going to be auctioned off on the docks in Hull. He had been informed there would be about 450 of them coming up for sale. Two weeks later I was at Hull's, King George Docks, attending the auction with Dad. He bought 400 of them for Coleshill Jim, for £22 each. They were all brand new and were still in their boxes, and were in two tone, red and grey colours. I think a car dealer from Hedon bought the remaining 50.

250 of them were delivered to Jim in Coleshill by a fleet of trucks, but before they were even unloaded, Jim had lined up a customer in Holland, who sent a bank transfer through to him to pay for them, so the trucks turned round and brought them all the way back to Immingham Docks, to be shipped out, to Holland.

Dad was asked by Coleshill Jim to sell the other 150 for him. A motorcycle dealer came from Doncaster and bought 40 of them for £38 each then Dad sold the remaining 110 over the next three months for £49 each. The dealer from Hedon's selling price was £69 each, so Dad sold out first. This was a lesson to me on how you can sell large amounts of brand new bikes if the price is right, and this observation would come in very handy for me, one day in the future.

There was a guy in Hull who was a Velocette fanatic called Geoff Chapman. He and his brother rode in scrambles and grass tracks. Dad had arranged for Geoff to go with us to a scrambles meeting in Lincolnshire at a track near Caistor. Transport to the track was to be a Ford 10 van and trailer. Mine and Pete's two Matchless scramblers were loaded on to a newly acquired trailer, and Geoff's 350 Velocette scrambler went in the van, along with spare wheels, tool boxes, fuel and riding gear. Also in the van were me, Pete, Geoff and Burt with Dad driving. This all added up to a great deal of weight and the Ford 10 van didn't like it at all. It refused to do more than 35 m.p.h. flat out. The drive around the River Humber was about 80 miles and we eventually arrived at the track with about 10 minutes before the start of practice. I was 14 but filled my entry form out as 16 years old, and I was only able to do this thanks to Burt, for teaching me how to read and write, and nobody even thought to question my age as I was a big lad for only 14 years old.

Practice started. As this was my first actual race meeting to start with I just rode around following everyone else in order to learn the track. Practice lasted 10 minutes for the first session, and 15 minutes for the second session, and I stayed out as long as I could. The bike felt good, and I now much preferred the power of the 500cc engine to the 197cc Dot engine. The Matchless was a lot heavier but it was quite manageable.

The first race for me was the over 300cc race. Looking down the start line at the 18 other riders brought on a queasy feeling in my stomach, which instantly vanished when the starter dropped the start flag. Heading towards the first corner I reckoned I was in about eighth place, but on reaching it, I was amazed to see all the riders in front of me going out wide to get a swoop around the corner, so instead, I went straight down the inside and came out in third place. Geoff Chapman was leading, with a guy from Lincoln in second place. For three laps I just sat behind them following them round.

At the back of the circuit was a double jump, about 25 feet across. I had noticed everyone was riding through this jump, so I opened the Matchless throttle flat out in second gear, and made a suicide leap across the jump, and amazingly, landed safely in second place, totally startling myself and the guy from Lincoln, who was riding an AJS 18CS 500cc. He lost all interest in chasing the lunatic lad from Hull, who had just passed him by flying over his head. Gaining confidence, I followed Geoff for the next lap then, when we both reached the double jump again, went flying past him over his head. Rounding the last corner before the finish line I couldn't believe it when I saw the starter holding out the chequered flag. I had just won my first race and my brother Pete finished in sixth place.

Everybody went mad congratulating me when I returned to the pits. Burt pointed to the program and I discovered I had just won £5, but unknown to me, a stewards meeting was taking place at the start line. It seemed that three riders had complained that I had ridden dangerously. The stewards called me across to the meeting. There were two complaints against me they said, the first charge; cutting inside other riders on the first corner. The second charge; dangerously jumping over the double jump at the back of the circuit by going too high in the air. The two flag marshals who were stationed at these positions were also called into the discussion. Both said I wasn't riding dangerously at all, I was just taking a totally different line to the rest of the riders. The older of the two marshals actually said.

'I thought the object of racing was to pass the other riders, that's all Mason was doing' Both allegations were now dropped. Race two, the unlimited race started. At the first corner, again I just couldn't believe it, they were all still going out wide, so I went straight down the inside, tight up against the ropes, and came out in the lead. The double jump at the back of the track had now collected a large crowd of spectators. Word had got out that the loony rider from Hull, Nev Mason , was jumping right across the gap, about 10 feet high in the air. I must have gained about 50 feet a lap by doing this and won the unlimited race by a good quarter of a lap, while Pete got a seventh this time. Back in the pits there was a repeat of the congratulations, only this time the crowd was much bigger than before. When Burt passed me the program he pointed to 'Unlimited race - first place £10' My sums skills were not yet fully developed but I could calculate that would be £15. Somebody in the crowd around me and the bike shouted out.

'You're Mad Mason' and that was to became my nickname in scrambling for many years to come.

The third race was the all comers race with 28 riders on the line. This time I was 6th out of the first corner. I found the lads on the 200cc and 250cc two stroke bikes could take a much tighter line, because their bikes were lighter. By the 2nd lap I had managed to get up to 4th place. The guy in front of me was on a 200cc Francis Barnett and on reaching the double jump, on about the 7th lap, I was about 25 feet behind him. He had obviously decided that if I could jump across it so could he, but unfortunately for him, he didn't have the power of a 500cc engine underneath him, to launch him at speed across it . His low powered attempt saw him hit the bank at the far side of the double jump. As I took off I went right across to the left hand side of him. I saw him smack into the opposite bank, his bike breaking its frame and forks in half. My instinctive decision to go to the left on take off proved to be right, as I missed him and his two piece bike on landing. A bit further on I passed Pete who had also come a cropper and was out of the race. Now 3rd and with 2 more laps to go I finally got up to 2nd place. On the last lap I was about 250 feet from the finish line when I made a dive up the inside of the guy leading the race. I held the lead for about 100 feet from the chequered flag, but then my bike's back chain broke, and I ended up pushing the bike for the last 50 feet across the finishing line, coming in 3rd place. That's another £7, £22 total for the day. I had never had that much money that was actually mine.

Every thing was reloaded into the van and trailer and we began the return trip back to Hull. Going past Scunthorpe it began to rain very heavily. We had just driven on to the Gunness Bridge when the engine finally died out. All Ford vans of this period had black fabric roofs, and this one leaked badly. Rain water also some how got into the electric system of the Ford causing it to misfire badly.

Still heavily raining, nobody wanted to get out to dry the electrics, but Dad and Burt got out, lifted the bonnet and dried off the ignition leads and the distributor with a handkerchief found in the glove box. The engine eventually fired up and we were soon off the bridge, leaving behind a long queue of vehicles that had not been able to get past our van.

Going through Crowle a sudden gust of wind managed to get under the front of the fabric roof and it just vanished, it was last seen going across a field at high speed, scattering cows in all directions as it passed over their heads. What can you say in this type of situation. We all just sat there dismally looking at each other, and just when we thought things could get no worse it started to rain again.

Two hours later, five very wet, cold people complete with soaked equipment arrived back at Dad's garage in West Dock Ave. Me and Burt got out and opened the large double doors, and moved several bikes to the side of the garage to make room for Dad to drive the van and trailer inside, into the dry. Geoff's BSA 500 M20 and box sidecar was wheeled out of the garage and loaded up with his Velocette and equipment.

'Thanks for a very memorable day Albert' he said with a grin as he started up his M20 outfit and set off home with a wave. Shutting up the garage we all tramped the 100 yards to our house and luckily for us Mam had a good fire going and a large pan of chicken stew bubbling away on the range. Once warm and dry, full of chicken stew and fresh bread and with a large cup of tea, the events of the day were discussed. Pete and Dad begrudgingly admitted that they were surprised that I had won two out of the three main races. Burt chipped in.

'I did tell you Albert and Pete, that he was going fast now' This was a very special day that I would remember all my life.

Around this time, at aged fourteen, I started playing around modifying an old 1937 OK Supreme that was fitted with a 250cc JAP engine. Dad had bought it for two pounds so I gave him a pound profit on it and with Burt's help I stripped it down to the bare frame. We made up some alloy engine plates for it from quarter inch alloy plate, all hand cut with the help of a hacksaw and files. The frame was cut and re-welded at the back end to take a James rear swinging arm, back wheel and rear shocks, then the whole frame was fully repainted in bright red. The James telescopic front forks were fitted, as well as a twenty one inch front wheel, re-spoked by Burt and Avon scramble tyres were fitted back and front. An Excelsior 197cc petrol tank and a BSA seat were fitted then a pair of alloy mudguards finished it off. It looked a whole lot different now to what the standard bike looked like two weeks ago. I used to push this bike along the fish dock to the practice track at the end of the dock wall by the railway lines. I used this bike all summer and spent many happy hours on this track. The engine was quite quick and all the fun I had on the bike made it worth all the hard work that had gone into building it. My Matchless G80CS was now just used for serious practice at Melton and for racing in meetings. Just before Christmas a young guy from Anlaby came into Dad's garage and spotted my converted 250cc OK Supreme and asked if it was for sale. The net result was that the bike was sold to him for twenty six pounds. Dad got three pounds from the sale while Burt also received three pounds. I finished up with twenty quid in my pocket, **but I'd had a lot of fun and gained experience from building this bike.**

Nev Mason
saying
1959
If you believe in yourself and your capabilities then failure is not in the equation

Chapter 2

1958 was a year I don't really want to experience many times in my life. About six weeks after the meeting at Caistor, I opened up the garage at the normal time of 9 am, putting some bikes outside for display. I shouted to Burt but didn't get an answer. Going through to the workshop I noticed that the light was still on in his DIY bedroom. Burt lay on his bed, face down, still with his coat on, one arm hanging down at the side of the bed. He was obviously dead having died in his sleep. I was mortified and ran back home to get Dad. He came back out from the workshop area with tears in his eyes and picked up the phone to ring the police and explain to them what we had found. Burt was taken by the local undertaker to their rest rooms. Two days later his body was collected by his relatives and taken back to Pickering for burial. We were not invited to the funeral or even told when or where it would be. The sadness of this loss to me, lasted for years, he had been with us for over 3 years and he had become part of the family and my best friend. Things eventually started to return to normal, but didn't seem the same without Burt around.

Pete had an Ariel HS500 scrambler which I think came from Sid Desforges who was, as I remember, a real character who would burst out singing opera in the middle of talking to people. Dad did a fair bit of dealing with him and his two sons, Sid and Alan, who sold bikes and cars, and had a transport company at their yard in Witham, Hull.

Pete had gone out practicing on his newly acquired bike, but unknown to him, the oil pump had stopped working and this led to the engine seizing up. Over the next few weeks the bike had the engine removed and stripped, re-bored, new piston, new big end, and new cam and followers were fitted. Re-built, it was fitted back together and the bike was taken to Melton to run the motor in. Dad and Pete went in the garage's Austin pickup and on their return they were outside unloading the HS from the pickup when something happened. As the bike was being lifted from the back of the pickup, it slipped, and Dad, not wanting the bike to get damaged, grabbed it before it hit the floor. He saved the bike from any damage but injured himself.

Unknown to him or us, he had triggered off an aggressive cancer in his lower abdomen. This reduced him from his normal weight of eighteen stones to less than eight stones in five weeks. His resulting death at 42 years old, made it seem that life was not worth living. At his funeral I was amazed by the huge amount of people who came to pay their respects, not just from Hull but from all over England. His contacts had been many. Within the next few months the garage was empty, everything was sold. Pete had gone to work on the big M1 motorway project, driving an earth moving vehicle and Mam had gone to Corby, to look after her now terminally ill mother.

The end of 1958 could not come quickly enough for me. Not only was I grieving, I was left to look after myself in our house in West Dock Ave, though Mam made sure the £2 a week rent was paid. It's amazing what you take for granted in life. In the past, if I had wanted anything, I just asked Mam or Dad for it, but this normal, accepted privilege, had gone. For days I would sit alone in the house without coal for a fire or money to buy food. Definitely one of the low points of my life but, as they say, life goes on.

Next door to our house/shop was another house/shop which sold groceries, sweets, cigarettes etc. and luckily for me, Bill the owner saw my predicament and offered me goods up to the value of £1 a week, which he would record, and I would pay him back when I earned some money or got a job. I lived on bread and sugar sandwiches and packets of Camp coffee for months.

I was walking down Hessle Road one day, still feeling down in the dumps when a voice shouted out.

'Neville, hey Neville' It was one of Dad's friends, Albert Adams, who had a motorcycle shop on Anlaby Road. Dad often sold him bikes and he knew me quite well. He was delivering a bike to a house nearby. He asked.

'What are you doing now your Dad's gone?'

'Nowt' I answered.

'Why don't you come and work with me then?' he offered, so at 9 am the next morning I was waiting outside his shop. I had even had a cold bath the night before, it had to be cold as I didn't have coal for the fire to heat the water up.

I enjoyed working for Albert Adams, selling, and working on bikes for the next year. I paid off my grocery bill and managed to save £37. The last week I was there I clearly remember a guy walking into Albert's shop dressed in heavy motorcycle clothing.

Albert was out so I greeted him and made him a hot drink. He introduced himself as Peter Howdle. He had just started working for a newly established motorcycle paper called 'Motor Cycle News' which was to be distributed nationwide, and his job was selling advertising. Albert returned, but said it was of no interest to him, as he only advertised in the Hull Daily Mail, the local paper. The guy gave me his business card, because I told him I was leaving at the end of the week to start up my own motorcycle shop. He wished me well with my venture and rode off. Many years later I would renew my acquaintance with him through shows at Earls Court, NEC and road tests.

Now aged 16, I applied for and got a licence to drive a motorcycle on the road. At this time you could ride any capacity bike at 16, just stick L plates on it and off you went. You didn't even need to wear a crash helmet but I always did. £9 bought me a BSA M21, 600cc side valve, sidecar outfit, with a commercial box fitted where the sidecar should be, which had a drop down rear door at the back to help load the bike you were wanting to carry. The outfit had originally been owned and used by Miles Motorcycles in Hull for deliveries, I was told, but for the last two years a local builder had used it for carrying building materials and ladders. I spent a full day putting the bike into good working order, and fitting a new rear tyre and chain to it. This outfit was my transport for over five years and it never ever gave me any mechanical trouble. The insurance was £2.12s.6d per year, through Tullock's Insurance Brokers. A Mrs Sizer ran the office and I was a customer with her for over 22 years.

Now I had my own transport I was a able to go anywhere I wanted and it was a good feeling. The first week I went to Kidderminster, to an auction, only to find it had been on the day before I got there. Oh well, it was all experience and I enjoyed the long distance ride out, but after this I always checked dates carefully before setting off anywhere.

I lived on my own for over 18 months before Mam returned back home, after looking after Grandma two, as I called her, until she died and her affairs were sorted out. Pete also returned home about 3 weeks later, well loaded with money as he had been on about £40 per week, driving large earth scrapers on the M1 motorway contract, so life resumed some sort of normality, Mam even bought a TV set and a radio. For work, she opened the shop front of the house to sell clothes and shoes, both new and second hand.

Pete ordered a brand new Gold Star DBD 34 scrambler from Jordans, the big BSA dealer in Hull. It was ordered in full works specification and cost him £268. I remember drooling over it, displayed in Jordan's showroom window, after it had arrived in stock. I collected it for him on my BSA M21 outfit as he didn't have any transport at the time to carry it on.

That Saturday afternoon we took it up to the Hessle practice track, which was on the bank of the River Humber, at the end of St Andrews fish dock. Unloading the Goldie we fuelled it up and Pete rode it around the track. The sound of the bike made the hairs on the back of my neck stand up, it sounded brilliant. After twenty minutes Pete pulled up and asked if I wanted a go, his instructions were that I had to do no more than four laps on it. I jumped on and set off, and even though it was not my bike the feeling was unbelievable, only those who have ridden a brand new bike will know the exhilaration that I experienced.

I completed the four laps and pulled in. I began to collect my thoughts on the BSA. It really did handle and steer much better than the old 1955 500 G80CS Matchless I used to ride before Mam sold it, and although the BSA engine was a more revving engine, unlike the torque pulling engine of the Matchless, I thought that, all in all, the BSA was definitely a much better bike than the old Matchless was.

A two stroke cackled into life about a mile away and within a few minutes it was approaching the track. It turned out to be Gordon (Jeg) Butler from Hessle, another great character, who had been down to a Greeves dealer in Birmingham, Vale Onslow I think, and bought himself a new Greeves Hawkstone 250. The noise it made was absolutely deafening as the exhaust pipe consisted of a large open megaphone about fifteen inches long. Pulling up with a big grin on his face he asked.

'What do you think of this then, Masons?' then proceeded to tell us how he had hitch hiked all the way there, bought the bike, then managed to get a lift back to Hessle with the bike. It had taken him 2 days to complete the trip.

Me and Pete watched as he set off around the practice track at a fast, show off speed, too fast in fact, as it suddenly went deathly quiet around the back of the track. I set off running and Pete rode across. There was Jeg and his bike upside down in a large hawthorn bush. He had gone into a corner, far too fast, and ricocheted off an old derelict Bedford Van body and chassis that had been slowly de-composing for about 10 years. It was always everyone's intention to move this obstacle further from the track, but none of us ever got around to shifting it.

After 10 minutes we managed to extract rider and bike from the bush. We kicked it straight as best we could and Jeg slunk off back home to lick his wounds and recover his pride. The now very ex new, Greeves never did look pristine again, after its first lap wipe out. Pity that, I thought, I had hoped to get a few laps in on it.

Me and Pete spent the rest of the day running in the BSA engine until after about two hours, it ran out of petrol, so we loaded it back onto my M21 outfit and returned home. A passage ran down the side of our house, so to get the bike into the back yard to clean it, a lot of physical effort was needed. You had to carry the front of the bike, with the front wheel and forks in full lock, to get it down the narrow passage. We both set about cleaning the bike until it looked new again, then we had to carry it back along the passage again and into the front door so it could be stored in the back room of the shop where it was covered over.

Around this time I started buying second hand motorcycles, doing them up and advertising them for sale in the local newspapers. The best sellers at the time were ex army BSA M20's and ex army Norton 16H's. Most dealers didn't want them for some reason and I could buy them for between £1 and £5, for a really good one. I was selling them for between £8 and £10 each. Over the next year I must have bought and sold about 35 of them, enough to provide me with a reasonable living.

Pete's Gold Star stayed were it was for the next six weeks because he went back to the M1 project to help out with earth moving again, as they were doing some additional work on a motorway slip road. For six weeks it sat there, unused in the back room, and although I was tempted to take it out in Pete's absence, I managed to resist the urge. Pete finally returned from the motorway job and the first thing he did was take the covers off to check if I had been out on it.

I bought, from John Avery Motorcycles, a 1958 500cc, ex works Matchless G8O CS. The bike was an ex works Dave Curtis championship bike, which was really a much better bike than the 1955 version I had

Top: The ex Curt Jurgens Jaguar I bought
Bottom: BSA M20 I used to buy these for between £2 & £4

Top: 250 Dot Demon I owned for 1 week
Bottom: BSA Goldstar DBD32 I used and modified

received for my 14th birthday. I now started regularly going out to our local tracks practicing and I ran this Matchless engine for approximately seven years, and in all that time it only required one big end and two sets of piston rings, plus a gearbox main shaft.

At seventeen I started entering local scrambles, Sproatley, Roos, Scunthorpe, Retford, Armthorpe, Tunstall, Scarborough and Pickering etc., and found, apart from buying and selling bikes I could earn extra money scrambling. For three years I actually made an idyllic living this way. The Matchless, being an ex Dave Curtis works bike, was very fast and I can't think of many times it was beaten to the first corner.

Over the next few years, I modified the rear suspension to 9 inches movement, fitted a lightweight front wheel, Norton forks, and put the engine oil in the frame, alloy engine plates and a lightweight rear wheel. All this reduced the weight of the bike by 32lbs.

Now aged 21, I bought an ex Artie Radcliff DBD32 Gold Star . It was stripped down and the frame lightened, then I fitted it with Ceriani forks, I used this bike for two years and I got some good results on it Later I fitted my ex Dave Curtis works Matchless engine and AMC gearbox into the BSA frame. I sold the Gold Star DBD32 350 cc engine and the SCR gearbox taken from it, for £12. (Yes I know it makes me feel sick as well.) The bike was now also modified to carry the engine oil in the main frame tubes, an Ariel swinging arm and rear wheel was fitted the rear sub frame was cut off and shortened then the rear shocks were laid down for more suspension movement. I called this bike a Crossman in our Yorkshire and Lincolnshire centre meetings it proved to be just about unbeatable for about 3 years. I got the total weight on my Crossman 500cc bike down to 257lbs dry weight.

LESSONS IN LIFE

A major business lesson in life I learnt at the age of seven was never deal in anything that has legs, as it can run off. Dad bought me a new Raleigh push bike for Christmas which I swapped with a gipsy lad for his pet squirrel. The squirrel bit my fingers and ran off, never to be seen again. Net result - no squirrel and no bike.

Chapter 3

1963 brought a major change to my life, so there was something else in the world apart from bikes. Women. Pete was going out with a girl called Joy and one Wednesday afternoon she came to see Pete and brought her friend Valerie Meek with her. Val lived at Coltman Avenue, Beverley. Aged 18 she was a real looker. Pete and Joy were going for a drink on the Friday night and I was asked if I would like to take Val and go with them. The next day, I actually bought a new shirt to wear.

I can't remember what pub we went to that Friday but I got drunk on just two pints of Guinness and when we got home, I fell out of the taxi onto the pavement outside our house. I normally didn't drink alcohol so it had a profound affect on me. Val went home and the next day my head felt like it had been hit with a hammer.

'That's it' I thought 'won't ever see her again'. But on Monday night Mam came into the room and said.

'That lass Val is here to see you' Within a week we were seeing each other every evening after she finished work at Hammonds, the department store, where she was a cashier. After only a few months I proposed and luckily she accepted.

Four happy months passed by when she suddenly came out with the news that she was expecting a baby. Talk about a wake up call. I remember the next day I spent all afternoon sat at the North Ferriby practice track thinking.

'That's my scrambling career over' The end of the world seemed to have arrived, then I started thinking logically.

'Do I love her? Yes. Can I see myself spending the rest of my life without her? No. Do I want a son or daughter? Yes.'

The idea of having our own family together was the question that had just been answered. We were married at the registry office in Beverley, it cost seven shillings and six pence for the wedding certificate, that left me with £2 in my pocket.

I arrived on my M21 BSA sidecar outfit resplendent in a new (well sort of) suit from Mam's shop and the reception was at Val's parents house. I was not the most popular of grooms because I worked for myself. I recall Val's brother Victor asking where I

Top: Mine and Val's Wedding Day
Bottom: Family group at wedding

Top: Val and John
Bottom: John and Ian at Hull Fair

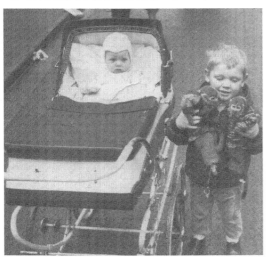

worked and when I told him that I was self employed he said.

'It must be nice to earn a living without working.' How totally naïve was he, self employed people put in far more hours than anyone who is normally employed would ever dream of doing. We lived at Val's parents house for about five months until John our first born was brought into the world in the back bedroom.

Val's mam asked for board money for our keep and when I asked.

'How much?' she replied

'£2 should cover it'.

'£2, Is that every week?' I asked.

'Yes, that's every week' I was told.

My Mam had taken a part time job working for Peter Burgess who had started a new firm in West Dock Avenue, specialising in re-lining truck brake shoes and supplying new hydraulic pipes etc. He bought a brand new Mini van which Mam used for his deliveries and he allowed her, at the weekends, to use it to take us to scramble meetings, and even had a tow bar fitted for pulling the bike trailer with.

We were at a scramble at Sproatley with our new

baby, John, who was comfortably ensconced in his cardboard, ex margarine box, which had been tastefully covered by Val, with pastel coloured, flowered wallpaper. This must have been an early prototype carry cot, only it didn't have handle straps, and had to be carried on your arms, but everybody gathered round to meet and inspect the Mason family's new kid.

I won all three races that day and took home £22 so we were financially secure for the next few weeks. I paid eight pounds to Val's mam from this money for the next month's board and bought a Triumph Tiger Cub for £3 from a house in Grovehill Road, Beverley and an Ariel Arrow Sports for £5 from Tickton. I advertised them from Val's parents house and sold them for £12 and £16. This didn't go down well with Victor, he seemed annoyed, to him it seemed too easy a way to make money.

After five months we moved to my Mam's house in West Dock Avenue as she didn't charge us any board money and things were starting to get a bit uneasy at Val's parents house. We stayed at Mam's for about a month then with the £28 maternity benefit Val received for John we opened a motorcycle shop at 624 Hessle Road which was quite successful. It had a flat above which became our first home of our own.

It was around this time, while practicing on the Hessle track a 17 year old kid called Geoff Stokes came into my life. Whenever I went practising the word went out that 'Mad Mason's coming' and all the riders, for some unknown reason, disappeared when they seemed to remember they had a more urgent appointment elsewhere. Stokes obviously hadn't heard the rumours about Mad Mason, or just didn't care, as he kept on going round the track on his BSA B31 350cc bike. I spent an enjoyable half hour hassling him to go faster round the track, which he did. He actually seemed to enjoy and appreciate it. After some weeks, he ended up working for me at my Hessle Road shop for, as I remember, £3 a week and two rabbit pies from the bakery down the road.

After about eight months we had £269 in the bank and everything was paid for, so I thought, as you do at that age that we had 'made it' and retired. We moved to a house on the bank of the River Humber near Barton in Lincolnshire, and Geoff moved with us. We rented the house for eight shillings a weeks (about 40 pence). This was how life should be; we got up every morning, had breakfast then went out with our bikes. The track was virtually in our back garden. In the afternoons we went rabbiting, rafting or fishing in the nearby lakes   After   six   months   we   all, surprisingly, got tired of this idyllic way of life. We had managed to live on £127 for the six months and returned, still with £142 in the bank, back to Mam's in Hull, but this was a bad move.

We had been back at West Dock Ave only for about 3 months when our second child was born, a boy we called Paul who sadly died shortly after birth with a heart defect. John was only 15 months old but we had wanted our family close together. Mam now seemed to think she could take over the running of John's life and made Val's life hell as she constantly interfered and insisted she knew best on how to bring up our baby.

It was time to leave again as we couldn't go on like this and we found, quite by accident, a house in Weel Road. Beverley. We had been passing and saw it was empty so knocked on the door of the adjoining house. Val had delivered papers there years before but the old lady remembered her and said we could rent it for 7s.a week and while we lived there, life was good. I could still win prize money from scrambling, and was buying motorcycles and selling them from Mam's shop in Hull. I bought a 250cc Dot but after riding a 500cc bike most of my life it was not fast enough so I sold it in our local paper

In 1966 I was at a big motocross at Boltby and I remember it well for three reasons. No. 1, in practice I passed 500cc champion, Jeff Smith and I led him for a full lap before he re passed me and then just disappeared. No.2, I was leading the 500cc experts support race when, on the last lap, the gearbox main shaft broke on my bike and No.3, it was at this meeting that Jerry Scott was sadly killed and the meeting was abandoned.

It was also about this time I bought two 80 ton ex British waterways barges that were moored up in a creek near to us. I paid £22 for both of them and within 4 days had managed to get £27 back from the brass and copper fittings they had on them. It was almost like having my own bank as they now stood me to nothing, in fact I was £5 ahead. Every time money started to get low I just got out my cutting gear, went down and spent a day cutting 3 foot by 2 foot pieces off them using oxy-propane.

At that time, this type of scrap was fetching about £6 a ton. When I had accumulated about 8 tons of cut scrap a wagon would come from Thomson's of Hull and collect it and take it to their scrap yard. Cutting them up for scrap over the two years we lived at Weel Road provided some extra income which bought more bikes.

We tried again for another baby and Ian was born during this period. We were extremely happy for a while but this was to be cruelly dashed. When he was about three months old we were told he had a hole in his heart and had little chance of living to adulthood. We moved from Beverley to De Grey Street in Hull to live in 1967. Ian was 6 months old and had regular trips to the Hull Royal Infirmary. About a week before he would have been 9 months old Val was taking him by bus to visit my mam. He caught a cold from another child sitting opposite on the bus and was not strong enough to fight it off. He went into hospital on New Years Day and died on 4th January 1968. It was too traumatic for words.

During the time we had lived at Weel Road, Beverley I collected quite a few bikes and when we moved to De Grey Street in Hull I opened a motorcycle shop at the bottom of West Dock Ave which gave me a base to sell the accumulated bikes from. This shop was quite successful and within 3 months I was having to go to Grimsby, Scunthorpe and Doncaster to find stock to sell. In 1968 I rebuilt the ex works Matchless G80CS engine fitted in my modified BSA Crossman frame and then sold the bike to a guy from Sheffield.

This is also the year I passed my car driving test, after two attempts with Quick Pass in Hull who ran a fleet of Minis. A Morris Minor pickup then became my transport as it was ideal for carrying bikes and for general use. The old BSA sidecar outfit which had served me well for many years was sold for £25 so it managed to generate £16 profit even after all the years of use.

In this year I also bought a brand new Sprite 360 which handled very well and was quite quick and light, but the left hand kick start lever was placed in such a position that it constantly rubbed on my leg. Out practicing at Ferriby one day I got tired of this and moved the folding metal stub part behind my leg. Later, going over a jump, my foot slipped off the footrest and onto the ground, but now my leg couldn't go backwards because of the folding stub being behind it and the result was one broken leg. Slowly I came to a stop and laid the bike down on the right hand side. I had never had a broken bone before but I didn't need telling what had happened. Luckily I was not at the practice track on my own and somebody, went for an ambulance. The track was about one and a half miles from the road and I was carried back all the way to the road on a stretcher, by the none too pleased ambulance men, who took me to the Hull Royal Infirmary where I was told I had broken both my Tibia and Fibula. I was put into a plaster cast up to my groin.

After two months of inactivity I bought a silver Jaguar mark two 2.8 with an automatic gearbox so at least I could get about again, by driving around with my left leg stuck out and using just my right leg on the controls. I later cut my plaster down to just below knee level. This was so I could go out practicing on my bike. I went out three times on the Sprite with the trimmed down plaster with my toes sticking out of the end and Val would spend ages picking the thistles out of my toes every time I came home from riding. I recall it took me many months to walk properly again, because when the plaster was finally removed, my left leg was about 35% smaller than my right leg and felt very weak.

I sold the 360 Sprite and bought a 441cc Cheney Victor, but the duplex frame was too stiff, with no give in it. A later Cheney Victor I bought, was fitted with the single down tube frame and this was a lot better for my style of riding. I part exchanged the duplex framed Cheney for a CZ 360 twin port which I ran for about nine months and I had some good results on this bike.

At around this time we had a fourth baby boy, Alan, who unfortunately had the same heart condition as Paul and Ian and he also died. We decided we could not risk having more children. A few months later we were approached and asked if we would be interested in adopting a baby. We were delighted to do this and made a full legal adoption when Deborah was born and she happily completed our family.

Because of what had happened to our boys I decided to go for a medical check up at the hospital and they found that I'd had a defective heart from birth, with an irregular heart beat, arterial fibrillation, and a heart that was twice the normal size. It would seem that by doing years of scrambling, this had made my heart very much enlarged but had also made it very strong. My heart beat at this time was about 30 to 40 beats per minute. Years of racing had made it a large strong slow pump. I was told by all the doctors that I would be lucky if I reached 30 years old, and my heart problem was obviously one of the reasons for our babies heart defects.

This long term inbuilt condition had also affected my racing in scrambles and MX more than I had realised. Twenty minute races were usually no problem for me, but thirty or forty minute races sometimes finished up with me being totally breathless, only the will to finish the races kept me going. At least now I knew why I was getting so breathless in the long races and what the problem was. I cannot complain as I am now 69 years old and so far have beaten all the Doctors estimations of my life span by 39 years.

HOW MUCH? I WANT TO SELL THE BIKES TO YOU NEV NOT PAWN THEM.
QUOTE FROM FREDDY FRITH HONDA GRIMSBY.

Nev Mason saying 1968
When people say it can't be done that should give you the motivation to prove it can be done.

Chapter 4

In 1968 I rented an additional shop in Woodcock Street, Hull. This shop was bigger than the West Dock Ave shop. I had a lad helping me run the West Dock Ave shop, Mark McKay, who was a brother of one of the Hessle Road Mafia, and was nick named for some odd reason 'Mickey the Mouse' (he looked more like a rat to me than a mouse). Mark had a good interest in bikes and was a good worker and trustworthy.

One day at the new Woodcock Street shop a little Indian guy came in and spent 10 minutes going over every bike in the shop under 125cc. I asked could I help him.

'No I'm just looking, can my friends come in to look at them?'

'OK' I said not really knowing what else to say. About a minute went by then he came back into the shop beckoning to nine more of his Indian mates to come in. They all spent time checking out the bikes and a meeting was called by the first guy, over in the corner of the shop, it was like a rugby scrum, and they all jabbered away with much arm waving. Finally it went quiet and stepping forward the spokesman, in perfect English asked me.

'If we buy many bikes would they be cheaper to buy? '

'Yes' I replied. They had an interest in 6, 50cc Mobylettes, 2, 50cc NSU Quickly's, 1, James 125cc, 1, Excelsior 125cc, 3, 100cc Capri scooters and 1, 50cc Raleigh Wisp. I asked them for 5 minutes while I worked out some prices for them. I concluded the 14 bikes had cost me to buy in, a total of £103. I asked them £225 for the lot and they had a quick jabber and more arm waving and then the spokesman put forward an offer of £240 for the lot, if I delivered them to the docks for them. I accepted as this was not a bad profit for the day. The head man then asked if I could deliver them straight away as they were sailing later that night for Mumbai.

There was a guy who lived opposite the shop who collected scrap with an old Morris Commercial, 3 ton truck. To cut a long story short I gave him £4 to borrow his truck and it was loaded up with the 14 various mopeds and scooters. The head guy Dinesh, as his name turned out to be, climbed into the truck with 2 of his mates leaving the rest to find their own way back to the ship.

Climbing into the borrowed truck, and directed by Dinesh, I drove them through Hull and onto King George Dock. The police stopped me at the dock entrance and asked me.

'Where are you going with all this lot?' pointing to the pile of bikes on the back of the truck.

'I'm delivering these bikes to their ship' I answered,

'That's OK then' he said and waved me through. Dinesh directed me to an absolutely massive cargo ship moored at the east end of the dock.

'First Mr Nev,' as he insisted on calling me. 'Please come with me on to the ship and I will pay you for the bikes before we unload them' This was one of those situations where you think.

'What have I let myself in for?' It seemed to take forever going down the dimly lit stairs which descended to the bottom of the ship. Right in the ship's bilges was their living quarters, bunks everywhere, there must have been about 40 of them. In their cramped living space Dinesh asked me to sit down as he pulled a big black trunk out from under his bunk and counted out £240 in grubby notes to pay for the bikes, and then thanked me for delivering them to the ship for him.

I sold Dinesh many more mopeds and bikes during his trips here over a period of about 18 months. Then some new regulations came out in India and Dinesh could no longer take any bikes back there. This lucrative gravy train had now stopped.

I had part exchanged my CZ 380 for a new Greeves 380 Griffon twin port and I rode this bike for about a year and really enjoyed it. I had some good results on it but I then made a major mistake, when I part exchanged it for a new 250 Greeves Griffon, at the end of the year. This bike was not fast enough to pull my now 16 stone weight about so I sold it.

It was around this time I had to give up the West Dock Ave shop because the chicken factory, which was located behind it, bought the building so they could use it to extend their factory. Mark also left at this time to return back to trawlers. It was no real problem as the Woodcock Street shop was big enough and doing well.

Reading the Hull Daily Mail one evening I saw a Mark 2, 3.4 Jag for sale. The previous owner was Kurt Jurgens the German film star, and the car was finished in gleaming white with all manner of extras fitted. The registration number, as I remember, was

EYO 46. and it had a tow bar fitted to it. I bought it for £395, and at the same time bought a four wheeled car trailer for carrying bikes on, which I kept for over 12 years. I wouldn't like to estimate how many bikes it carried in this time.

I had driven to Selby to pick up two Honda CB92's I had bought, they had been repossessed from a company that had gone into liquidation. I collected the paperwork from the office and was asked if I would be interested in buying a bankrupt motorcycle shop's entire stock of bikes, plus the workshop equipment and spares etc. The guy from the office took me round to show me what was for sale, as the shop was within walking distance. He opened the rear door and on entering, to me, it was like walking into Aladdin's Cave. Packed inside was what one guy had collected for 32 years. Trying very hard not to look too interested I had a good look round at what was to be cleared out. The guy told me they had sold the property and it had to be cleared out within one week. On returning to his office his boss shouted out.

'Well are you interested in clearing it all out or not?'

'How much do you want for it all?' I asked him

'It's eight hundred quid for the lot' he snapped. back. I didn't like his arrogant attitude so I shouted back.

'Sorry I'm not interested' I left my card on his juniors desk and walked out. I had just taken a calculated gamble knowing that they had only a week to clear it all out. I had just got into the Jaguar when the office junior came running up and knocked on the window. Apologetically he enquired what I would offer for it all.

'£600 for the lot, that's the maximum' I said. 'Give me a ring if he changes his mind'.

'Please hold on for 5 minutes while I go back in to speak to him again.' True to his word he came back out in five minutes complete with a bill of sale for the entire contents made out to me for £600 for everything. I gave him a cheque for £600 and £5 for himself and I started to clear it out the next morning with a new helper. We worked flat out, taking 11 trailer loads of bikes and gear back in 4 days to the Woodcock Street shop.

The bikes were 2 x Matchless Twins, 3 x BSA 250 C15's, 1 x BSA A10, 2 x BSA A7's, 1 x AJS 500, 2 x Tiger Cubs, 1 x Roland Pike road racing Gold Star,

2 x Ariel Leaders, 1 x Ariel Sport, 1 x Ariel Square Four, 2 x Norton ES2's, 1 x Norton Dommy 600, 1 x John Tickle equipped Triton, 1 x Triumph 3T, 2 x Garrelli Mopeds, and 3 x Mobylette mopeds plus about 3 tons of second hand and new spare parts, 14 new helmets, 6 pairs of new motorcycle boots, 7 fibreglass top boxes, the list just went on and on. Needless to say the Woodcock Street shop was stuffed full. I even had to take three trailer loads of gear back home to my De Grey Street house to store it.

On the Monday morning I found out through a contact, that 2 new BSA B50 M X's were being used in a Sydney Poitier film. One was for stunts, the other just for static shots. I bought them both after the film was completed and ran them for nearly two years using one as a practice bike and the other purely for racing.

The Roland Pike Gold Star was a beautiful bike. I advertised it in Motor Cycle News and a guy rang me from Holland. He had a small collection of Roland Pike machines so, in response to my advert, came across with his German friend to view it. Both guys spent about an hour going from front to back, gleefully looking all over the bike. The guy called Jon asked me.

'Do you know which Pike bike this is?' Not

really understanding him, I said I didn't understand the question. He asked me.

'Did you know this was one of his most famous Gold Star bikes?' I didn't, (well you can't know everything). I had advertised the bike 'open to offers' but even I was surprised when he asked if I would take £350 for it. Mmm I had to stop and think about that. Tongue in cheek I answered.

'No sorry, its got to make at least £375'

'OK I'm happy to pay you that' he said, immediately leaving me thinking this guy definitely knew something I didn't about this bike, but as I had given only £600 for the Selby shop's entire stock of bikes and parts I told myself not to be greedy and shook his hand to seal the deal.

His German friend had taken an interest in the John Tickle Triton and asked me in pigeon English, how much it was.

'I want £150 for it.' I managed to convey to him. Jon and his friend talked together for a few minutes, then Jon who spoke good English took over and said his friend would give £120 for the bike. I was now thinking, £375 and £120, that's £495 for two bikes so I will have £105 in everything else from Selby (That'll do me). Jon paid for both bikes from a huge wad of notes he had in his briefcase. I gave him a receipt for the two bikes so they could show customs that they were his property, and they loaded them on to their VW pickup.

Interestingly enough, about a year ago in 2010, I saw the same Pike Gold Star advertised for £12500, and I thought I had done well out of it. It just goes to show how values have increased .

In 1971, I built John, my now 7 year old son, who had been pestering me for about a year now, a bike using a Honda C100, cut down and fitted with Capri 80 scooter wheels, so he could reach the floor. I had previously built him a small scrambles push bike, with front suspension and rear cantilever suspension, which he terrorised all the local kids in De Grey Street on, but he now wanted something with an engine. When his new mini bike was finished, me and Marty took John to the Hessle practice track. Starting it up for him, we showed him how the controls worked, then put it into first gear and the rest, as they say is history. He opened the throttle wide, the auto clutch kicked in and he was gone. After 30 seconds I realised I couldn't keep up with him so Marty took over running at the side of him, issuing instructions on how to stop if he wanted to. John didn't want to stop, this was far too exciting to stop, and he soon out paced a puffing and panting Marty and disappeared out of sight down the track. I ran to my BSA B50 MX which was stood at the side of the Moggy pickup, started it up and was just about to set off to look for him when he arrived back, full of smiles, he grabbed a big hand full of front brake then fell off the bike. It was a good job he had a helmet on. He was very quick to get up and excitedly proclaimed.

'That was great fun can I go round again Dad?' Oh dear, not another scramble bike convert I thought to myself.

NEV MASON, A BLUNT AND DIRECT AND VERY VERY CLEVER YORKSHIRE MAN AND A SOMEWHAT UNRECOGNIZED GENIUS IN THINGS TWO WHEELED.
QUOTE FROM SEAN PEPPER, SAAB CARS, HULL.

Chapter 5

In late 1971, I shut the Woodcock Street shop and started trading with just dealers. Gallagher's, the Hull fairground people operated a go kart track at the seaside town of Hornsea and they were looking for someone to take it over as they were not being very successful with running it, mainly because of their lack of mechanical understanding of the karts. When asked if I would be interested in taking it over I went one Sunday to gauge if it was a viable proposition. The so called karts they were operating must have weighed about 5 cwt each and were powered by industrial engines which were not suitable for the job. After watching for about two hours I came to the conclusion that there was potential in it, simply by the amount of custom they were losing. They were running 10 of these so called karts but at any one time only 4 or 5 were actually in working order as they were continually breaking down. The track rent was £2000 per year, payable to Hornsea Council and Gallaghers had paid £1000 for the first part of the year. If I decided to take it over they said they would just walk away. The main days for the track were Saturday and Sunday, which would scupper my MX riding, so all the family went home to give it some thought.

As I had shut the shop and was trading bikes with other dealers during the week I wasn't tied to sitting in a shop everyday, and this gave me a big element of freedom compared to before. This new method of selling bikes could continue, and as I was now approaching 30, I didn't take scrambling too seriously any more, so the decision was made to take over and run the track on Saturdays and Sundays.

Gallagher seemed very relieved when I told him I would take the track over, but only if he gave me £500 towards building 10 new karts, and left all the other equipment on site. The deal was done and dusted. I spent all of the next two weeks building new karts and fitted them with Honda C100, 50cc, four stroke engines with auto clutch and time proven reliability. They proved to be the ideal choice for the job. It took three weeks to finish making all the 10 new karts, which actually looked like karts and weighed about a third of the previous contraptions.

The first Sunday we opened at 9am was mega. All the karts ran faultlessly throughout the day and we finished operating at dusk. I really enjoyed the year

The Kawasaki I modified

My first B50 MX 500

operating the kart track and it paid quite well but in October, at the end of the season, two local Hornsea guys, John Bailey and Adrian Wake asked me if I was interested in selling them the track and karts. Though I had enjoyed it, the answer was yes and they bought the lot and ran it successfully for the next few years.

Now free of having to operate the track every weekend I started riding again at scrambles meetings. What puzzled a lot of people was the fact that having not ridden in meetings for over sixteen months I could still run with the other top riders in the area. I found out they weren't going any faster while I had been away from moto cross, as everybody was now calling the sport.

It was now back to MX and I was running a BSA, B50, MX 500 and I got some good results on my return. Geoff Stokes and Rodney Harrison were now the quickest riders in the area and were at my come back meeting at Scarborough, I fully expected that both these riders would have significantly improved in my absence over the last 14 months.

In the first 500cc final I just sat behind Geoff for the full race following about ten feet behind, just to let him know he couldn't shake me off. He was a close friend and I know if I had gone out of my way to beat him after not racing for so long he would have sulked for a month.

Next in the allcomers final I repeated the same procedure, just to sicken him off. In the main race of the day he shot off in the lead and made a very determined attempt to put some space between us. Unfortunately for him I had mentored him for many years so I knew exactly what his plans were. I just sat on his back wheel again and passed him, on I think, lap 5 or 6 at the bottom of the track, just to let him know I could if I wanted to, and then let him past again. It was nice to know he was not going any faster in my 16 month absence. Anyway, my point was now proven. Geoff knew, that I knew his capabilities.

What I had discovered with Geoff, many years before was that he only had one top speed, in wet or dry conditions he used the same tempo. When it was dry I could always stay with him, no problem, but when it was wet and muddy, I would confidently say he was amongst the top 5 fastest wet weather riders in the UK, at his peak. His long legs and extremely good balance, and the fact that he always rode sat down gave him a unique style in the wet.

Geoff always took racing far more seriously than I ever did. I remember a particular Moto Cross meeting at Scunthorpe. During the unlimited final, I was leading and Geoff was second while his best mate and brother in law, Adrian Thompson was fifth. Adrian came off his bike on the back straight at high speed and as I came round I could see that he was in a bad way, so I stopped, parked my bike up and helped the ambulance men to move him from the track and put him into the ambulance. Geoff, on the other hand, decided to make the most of this opportunity and carry on to win the race. This must have been more important to him than it was to me. It took me a lot of years to truly discover just how selfish a person he really was, but that's another story, as they say that's how life is.

I got back to the business of motorcycles on the Monday morning. I got on really well with Henry Hall, no not the band leader, this Henry Hall owned Cushworths of Doncaster. He was a great guy to deal with and I bought and sold a lot of bikes with him. Other great characters I had years of dealing with were Doug Hacking, who owned the Kawasaki Centre in Bolton, Bill Brown in Cumbria, Freddy Frith in

Grimsby and Derek Cook the Datsun car dealer. These were all great guys who shaped my business life for years to come. All were very influential in many decisions I was to make in the motorcycle business. Doug had recently become a dealer for CZ moto cross bikes, so on one trip to his shop I bought 3 new CZ 400's and 2 new CZ 250 motocross bikes from him.

By this time I was running a VW pickup and trailer, having sold the 3.8 Jurgens Jaguar to a guy who had a ride at the go kart track. He'd asked if the Jag was mine, then he asked if I wanted to sell it. I told him.

'If you're interested give me a bid, if you bid enough you'll buy it if you don't you won't.' He said.

'I'll give you £550 for it.' but I said,

'If I'm going to sell it its got to make £600.' He then wanted to know if there was any chance that he could go for a drive in it. I said there wasn't, but I would take him myself for a quick five minute spin round Hornsea. On our return he asked for my address so that he could collect it and, sure enough, at 9.30 the next morning there was a knock on my door when the guy turned up to collect the Jag. Asking him into the house I got Val to make out a receipt while he counted out the money. He paid for it in cash, and I gave him the log book and keys and went outside with him. He started it up and disappeared down the street. I only ever saw the car again once, about five years later, parked in a car park in central Hull.

A local carpet firm at the top of De Grey Street had a VW 1400 van for sale which I bought for £245, so I sold the VW pick up and I ran this van for about three years, covering thousands of miles with it. It performed well without any problems.

Of the new CZ scramblers I bought from Doug Hackings I kept one for myself and sold the rest. The bike I kept, after I had modified the rear suspension and many other parts to make it lighter, performed ok. I sold it at the end of 1972 when I bought 4 new Kawasaki 400cc scramblers from Doug Hacking. Again I kept one for myself and sold the rest.

I modified it for the 1973 race season by fitting it with long travel Marzocchi front forks, altering the rear suspension to give it 9 inches travel, and lightening it off by 12lbs. The biggest problem I remember with this bike was its gear box, which stripped two third gear pinions, and the vibration from the 400cc air cooled engine was very bad.

At the time I'm writing this story it is late 2011, and I have recently seen, advertised the very same bike that I modified and raced all those years ago. I think it made £1500 on Ebay, which is a lot more than the £324 I paid Doug for each of the four brand new Kawasaki KX 400's .

IN THE MOTOR CYCLE TRADE THE MORE SUCCESSFUL YOU GET THE MORE JEALOUS YOUR ENEMIES SEEM TO BECOME OF YOU.
QUOTE FROM DOUG HACKING KAWASAKI BOLTON.

LESSONS IN LIFE

I was once offered a Jaguar XK120 for seventy pounds but turned it down because I thought it was too expensive, another time I was offered a Brough Superior with a V Twin, Jap engine, for forty five pounds, and yes again, that also was too expensive, or so I thought at the time. They do say you get wiser as you get older!

Nev Mason saying
If you are enthusiastic about what you do, this enthuses the people around you

Chapter 6

It was around this time that I first met Alan Voase who was to become my business partner in Neval Motorcycles for many years to come. The name Neval came from *Nev*ille and *Al*an. We couldn't think of anything else at the time so that's what it became. Across the road from my house was a café which I'd had my eye on as a possible future motorcycle shop, so when the café closed and the property became vacant I rang the agent and was told it would cost £500 to buy freehold. This all happened in the same week I met Alan, so I gave him a ring and when he arrived we went across the road to inspect the premises and weigh up if it was suitable to sell motorcycles from. It needed a lot of work to make more room but we decided to buy it.

We put £250 each in to buy the shop, then another £250 each for stock. We spent about three weeks knocking walls out and generally making more room inside, then we erected a large shed in the back yard of the shop for storage and finally it was all finished. All we had to do now was buy some bikes and start selling them.

First stop was Doug Hackings where we bought 3 second hand scrambles bikes. On the way back we called in at Bob Allports Honda Centre at Thorne as he had previously telephoned me to say he had some bikes for sale. After about 2 hours haggling we bought 3 crashed Honda C50's and a clapped out BSA 441 Victor. It's amazing what you can fit into a Volkswagon van. We drove slowly back to Hull with seven bikes in the back.

Alan stayed in the shop for the next few days working, with Marty helping to sort out these seven bikes, getting them ready for sale while I went out buying again. This time I went to Cushworths of Doncaster and came back with two Honda 90's, a BSA Bantam, a Suzuki TS 125 Trail bike and a Garelli Rekord Moped. This gave us a starting stock of twelve bikes to sell. A Lintek rep called in and we bought some helmets, boots and oils etc. to help fill out the shop.

The following week, Hull Daily Mail carried our first advert for the new shop. It's at moments like this you start to think 'Have I done the right thing?' Probably Alan was thinking just the same, but I never asked him. The advert was in the paper on the Friday night and we opened the shop on the Saturday morning at 9am. Within three hours we had sold four bikes. It was busy all day, we couldn't possibly have had a better opening day.

Monday morning dawned and we were stood in an almost empty shop again. Mmm I think we need some more bikes, was the general opinion. Marty looked after the shop while me and Alan jumped into the faithful VW and headed out of town to find more stock. On the long uphill drag out of Hull on Boothferry Road, I was amazed to see, in my mirror, that Alan was fast asleep on the engine cowl at the back of the van. I soon learned, in the many years we were in business together, that he could sleep just about anywhere.

Calling in at dealers in Goole and Knottingley, all places I had visited before, we bought a total of eight bikes, then headed back home to find Marty had sold another bike in our absence. The format, for the next six months was almost always the same. Monday and Tuesday we would go out buying stock, Wednesday and Thursday we prepared the bikes for sale and Friday and Saturday we sold the stock. Every Monday we stood in an almost empty shop, so we climbed in the van and off we went again. What we needed were more bikes and a second shop.

I have always found in business that when opportunities come up, you not only have to be in the right place at the right time but you have to recognise them. D C Cooks at Doncaster, the big Datsun dealer, had decided to go into the motorcycle market in a big way. They had opened a Kawasaki Centre in Doncaster and a Honda Centre at Goldthorpe near Doncaster. I watched their progress with much interest and reports filtered back to me that they were selling a lot of new bikes and taking a lot of second hand bikes in part exchange, in fact they were beginning to overflow with them. I called in to see Henry Hall at Cushworths and he confirmed that Cooks were selling a lot of new bikes. He had worked out that the strategy of D C Cooks was to sell new bikes at absolute top prices, gaining them a maximum hire purchase commission rate from the finance company, which allowed them to give over the top part exchange allowances on the bikes they took in.

I went to Doncaster Kawasaki Centre and asked to see Mr Cook but I was firmly told that this was not possible as he didn't see people without an appointment. Changing tactics I asked the smart Alec.

'How long have you worked for D C Cooks?'

'About two years' he growled back.

'Does he pay you well?' I asked

'You must be b——y joking, pay me well, that's a laugh'

'Kevin' I said. He looked very surprised that I knew his name perhaps he had forgotten he was wearing a badge with his name printed on it.

'Kevin' I repeated, 'How would you like to earn £50 cash?' Suddenly I had his undivided attention.

'Get me an appointment today with Cookie himself and there's £50 cash in it for you.' Forty minutes later I was stood in Cookies office. Never the best of dressers I was wearing the old sheepskin jacket I had worn for many years, and a scruffy pair of jeans. After introducing myself he grudgingly acknowledged that he had heard of me.

'I have been told' I said 'that you have a lot of second hand bikes for sale.'

'Yes I have' he said 'but I'm only interested in finding someone to take the lot, every week as we aren't geared up to selling used bikes, we concentrate on selling new bikes.' We talked for a while and I agreed to buy all the second hand bikes from his Doncaster Kawasaki Centre and Goldthorpe Honda Centre for the next two years. I arrived back at our shop in De Grey Street a bit like Neville Chamberlain with a signed piece of paper from Hitler, only my piece of paper was signed and dated by Mr D C Cook. Alan looked at it in horror.

'How much is this going to cost us?'

'A lot' I replied 'Anyway I haven't actually bought any bikes yet I've got to go tomorrow and bid for the first lot' Working out that with the £4000 in the bank and an £8000 overdraft facility we could raise £12000. Alan's dad said he would lend us some money if we needed it.

The next day I went to the Kawasaki Centre first where they had 32 second hand bikes in stock at that time. I knew that when Cooks took bikes in part exchange, they checked them over with a fine tooth comb, making sure they didn't end up with bikes that needed any work doing to them. This meant that I didn't have to go down the line of bikes checking out each individual one mechanically, as this had already been done by Cooks.

Walking in I saw Kevin who, by his response

when he saw me, had been told about the deal I had done with Derek Cook. There was a long line up of second hand bikes down one side of the showroom, so, note book in hand, I went along the line writing down the registration numbers of each bike and what make and model it was. Completing the list I sat down and calculated the book prices on each bike then totalled them all, then cut the total. You can buy anything cheaper if you buy in quantity, that's the same format in any trade. The book price was £8200 so I wrote down £5250 for the lot. Kevin rang Cookie up and told him I wouldn't bid a separate price for each individual bike, I had just given him a block bid for the lot. Derek asked how much I had bid and when he was told £5250 he said that it was OK but Kevin had to get a cheque from me there and then. I wrote a bank cheque out and loaded 16 of the 32 bikes into the VW and trailer saying that I would be back in the afternoon to pick up the other 16 bikes.

When I got back to our shop we had to put some bikes into the shop and some in the back shed and after a quick bite to eat I returned to the Kawasaki centre and loaded up the remaining bikes. I made sure I collected a bill of sale listing all the makes, models and registration numbers and a log book for every bike and got back to the shop at about 6.30 pm. Alan had stayed on and with a struggle we eventually packed all the bikes in somehow. 32 bikes doesn't sound a lot but believe me it is when trying to pack them into a small shop and rear shed. Alan couldn't quite believe I had bought them all for, £5250.

The next day Alan went with me to Goldthorpe where they had 22 bikes. I followed the same format I had used at the Kawasaki Centre but this time no one rang Cookie up and as the book prices came to £6140 I bid £4000 for the lot. The manager must have OK'd it because he appeared with a bill of sale with all the relevant information and log books. I wrote a cheque out and me and Alan started to load up the bikes. We managed to get 15 in and Alan returned later for the rest. Back at the shop we now had 54 more bikes in stock for an outlay of £9250 plus 7 left over from the previous week, 61 bikes. Nearly half had to be put in the back garden of my house as we couldn't get them into the shop.

One of the reasons we sold a lot of second hand bikes was because our prices were always about 20% lower than all the other Hull dealers. During the next week we sold 24 of the new stock from Cook's, which gave us some money back and some space for more bikes. We needed another shop rather urgently so bought a fairly big shop and yard in Calvert Lane at the other side of Hull and worked flat out to get it ready for use. We decided to call it TWOWHEELS. This shop had the bonus of a flat above it, which Alan decided to live in.

Over the next six months we had both shops running at full steam. We bought a lot of bikes from D C Cooks in this period and had a twin wheeled, Transit 30 cwt truck pulling the car trailer, carrying bikes back from Doncaster regularly three days a week. We must have been carrying by now one of the biggest stocks of second hand bikes in the UK and had to take on staff to cope with it. Derek Lockwood who now owns Spares Unlimited, Iain Lomax who is now an International Aircraft Captain, Dave Johnson who now specializes in rebuilding high class cars, Dave Jackson who now runs his own successful building concern, and became a life long friend, Dave Skelly, I don't have a clue what he is doing now, Sean Pepper, now owns his own garage specialising in Saabs. They all learnt a lot while working at Nevals over the years. More and more bikes were coming from D C Cooks as they expanded their sales so we had to expand our sales. Our business now became like pushing a snowball along it just kept getting bigger and bigger.

About this time, amongst one of the lots of bikes I bought from D C Cooks, was a Russian Minsk 125cc. I dragged it out, just out of curiosity, to have a look at it, never having seen one before. I spent an hour or so going right over it, starting it up and having a quick ride on it. It was better than I thought it was going to be. It was a bit rough round the edges but basically it wasn't a bad little bike. It was, as I was to learn later, based on the German DKW 125cc, which in England after the war, was developed into the BSA Bantam 125 cc for the English market. Anyway, observations over, I put it back in the large, recently erected shed in the back garden of my house. Where it stayed untouched for the next few months until another chapter in my business life developed from this bike.

It was now time to buy a larger shop so we bought 308 Beverley Road, Hull, a large ex Co-op shop. These premises were on a corner plot giving exceptionally easy access and it also had the advantage of a large warehouse at the back. The original Nevals

Top: Our TWOWHEELS shop
Bottom: Our NEVALS shop

Nevals stand at Birmingham show

name was transferred to this shop, but the De Grey Street shop also remained Nevals. We were still buying large amounts of bikes from Cook's Honda and Kawasaki Centres. We also started selling a lot of the late, big bikes to Cushworths, for good profit and it saved us carrying them back to Hull, however, as with all good things, they do eventually come to an end.

Cooks was going through a downturn in the market after their initial bumper 24 months of boom. The amount of bikes we were buying from them started to go down as their sales, and consequently their part exchanges slowed down. Now with three shops to keep going we were also buying from other dealers in the North. The Cooks contract had given us access to many, before inaccessible, large dealers, but as Cooks sales slowly went down and down there was still one last ace still in the pack.

It was Friday dinner time and I got a call from Derek Cook to ask me to meet him at Thurnscoe, that day. He had telephoned the shop and Alan had told him I was at Cushworths so it took me only about 20 minutes to get to the address he had given, which turned out to be a big old cinema building.

I met him outside and he said he had some bikes

to show me. He removed the padlock from the main door and I followed him inside. What a sight this was, there were bikes everywhere. He gave me four pages of hand written lists and told me that there were 227 bikes and he wanted a bid for the lot. I confirmed that I was interested, but I would need about 2 hours to go through them all. He had other business to attend to so he agreed to this and left me to it.

It was like putting a kid in a sweet shop, but down to business, I got my note book out and went round all the bikes on the list, checking them all out. I counted 222 second hand bikes, 5 short of his list. When Cookie returned he didn't seem very pleased about the 5 missing bikes but he asked me for my bid.

I had worked this out and was just about to give him the amount when he asked if I was interested in some new bikes as well. I said that I was and he took me to one side and pulling back some plastic covers revealing 5 new Honda CR125 Motocross bikes, 11 new Garelli mopeds, 12 new Mobylette mopeds, 4 new Garelli Tiger Cross Sports mopeds and 2 new Honda 50 SS Sports mopeds. All 34 new bikes were still in their boxes. He asked me to give him a bid for them all as well. Five minutes went by as I feverishly worked out a new total price for the entire 256 bikes. I bid him £35,000 for the lot, Derek then said.

'Another £5000 would buy them all.' he wanted £40,000. I had bid him £5000 lower, to allow him to push me up, so I was still getting them at my original figure. The only snag was he wanted them all moved out by Monday night and the only way I could do this was to hire two, seven and a half ton trucks, and get the full crew in to work Saturday, Sunday and Monday to move them all.

I wrote him a cheque for £40,000 and gave it to him as I left. He said that he would leave the keys with me if I would drop them in to him on Tuesday morning after clearing everything out. Everybody worked flat out over the weekend and Monday and by three pm on Monday afternoon we had everything cleared. I sold 16 damaged bikes from this lot to a good friend of mine, Mick Richardson of Temple Supplies in Hull. Mick brought his own transport to collect these bikes straight from the cinema building in Thurnscoe making it fewer bikes for us to move. As I understood it, all these second hand bikes at Thurnscoe were part exchanges from Cook's Datsun Car Centres. Amongst this batch of bikes were; 9 x Norton Commandos

850cc's, 5 x Triumph 750cc's, 3 x BSA A65's, 2 x 900 Ducati's, 4 x Suzuki GT 750 Kettles, 3 x Suzuki GT380's, 2 x Ducati 250's, 5 x Honda CB 500cc's, 1 x Kawasaki Z1000's, 3 x Kawasaki Z900s, 4 x Suzuki GT250's, 11 x Honda CB 250's, 3 x Honda CB 350's, 3 x Yamaha RD 350's, 3 x Yamaha RD 250's, 2 x Yamaha RD 200's, 7 x Honda CB125, 4 x Honda CB175's, 5 x Honda CD 175's, the list just goes on.

The Norton Commando's, Triumphs and BSA A65's were sold to Fred Wells, who was the original importer of Russian bikes into the UK before Satra Ind., the multi million pound, international company, bought the rights from him to take over the Russian M/C sales in the UK. Fred Wells was now specializing in S/H Norton's, Triumph's and BSA's. He flew up in his private plane, to Humberside Airport to check out the bikes and we delivered them to him in London the following week.

We still bought second hand bikes from Cooks, as and when they had them, but eventually both the Honda and the Kawasaki Centres closed down but we emerged from our Cook involvement very much better off financially than before we started dealing with them, and we had the three shops now all fully bought and paid for.

I was still riding in MX meetings as and when I had the time and I bought a new Suzuki TM 400. This was seriously, the worst contraption ever devised for MX. It looked like a copy of Roger Decoster's world championship bike, from about a mile away. It was the same nice bright yellow and black colour scheme but there the similarities stopped. In England the nick name for this bike became 'The Hospital Bike'. In the USA it was sold as a TM 400cc Cyclone and its nick name in the States was 'The Widow Maker'.

As I love a challenge I set out to try and tame it. The power was phenomenal but with no fly wheel effect, the power was like an on or off switch. The wheelbase was too long which gave it a pendulum effect and it viciously kicked out sideways at speed, you would find yourself suddenly going down the track backwards. The first thing I did was fit a one and a quarter pound flywheel weight onto the magneto. Next I cut the front frame top tube then butted the forks against a wall to bring the steering angle back, then welded in a 10mm piece of tubing to fill in the gap and welded another frame tube over the top to make sure it couldn't break. I fitted a Honda CD 175 swing arm to reduce the wheel base by 3 inches and made it a cantilever set up by welding on 20mm tubing to form the A frame. I then fitted a Citroen car adjustable shock with a spring from a tractor crop sprayer attachment and finally fitted a CCM rear hub and wheel and moved the footrests forward by 2 inches.

I took it out to our Hessle practice track to test it and suddenly with all the above modifications, and 31 lbs lighter and shorter, it was a totally different animal. When I modify a bike, it's achieved by my years and years of experience. If I can get the bike to safely do what I want it to do, then you can't ask anything more of it. The bike now turned well, was stable on fast straights and corners and the vicious engine power had been tamed by the fly wheel weight and the porting mods I did .

It was a winner the first time out at a Belchford TV meeting in Lincolnshire where it attracted much attention, as people were not used to seeing a Suzuki TM400 finishing a race, and many of them had certainly never seen one actually winning races. I ran this bike for about nine months, and got some very good results on it and it also turned out to be a very reliable bike.

Lincolnshire TV Cup I won on my
modified Suzuki TM400

Top: My Mam's back yard
Bottom: Day out at Whitby

Chapter 7

We took on an agency selling new Greeves motocross bikes, but the standard Griffon 380 was about past its best and not competitive anymore. I started to play around with one, and modified it to make it more competitive. We bought the bikes in standard trim from Greeves, made the modifications to make them more competitive then sold them. The carburation with the standard mono bloc carb fitted was absolutely terrible, so I fitted a Japanese Mikuni carb which was rubber mounted. This, plus a few porting mods completely transformed the engine characteristics. It now pulled like a four stroke from the bottom end to produce a wide range of power. Then I took the cylinder barrel down to only four cooling fins, as I had done on my earlier CZ 380s. The weight I removed from the Greeves barrel and head, on this original bike, was nearly 8 lbs. I cut the top frame tube, and gave it the wall treatment, to pull the fork angle back, then fitted a 9mm length of tube to the resulting gap and re welded it. This mod transformed the cornering as it was no longer raked out like a chopper. I laid the rear shocks down and strengthened the sub frame. The rear shocks I used were Husqavana type Girling gas shocks. Again a CCM rear wheel was fitted which was 6 lbs lighter than the Greeves rear wheel. I fitted an alloy seat base which saved another 3lb over the Greeves steel seat base, and lengthened the front fork movement by 2 inches, and converted them to air action instead of springs. Another 3 lb gone. Of all the many different standard bikes I modified, this one turned out to be one of the best bikes to ride, it did everything you ever asked of it.

A Mr Ralling rang from Greeves to ask if I would take my converted Greeves with me, when we went to collect more standard bikes we had on order with them, so they could have a look at it. We went the following week taking my modified Griffon 380 with us as requested. When we got there it was wheeled into their workshop so they could examine it while me and Alan were invited to lunch with two of the Greeves directors, Derri Preston Cobb and a young, tall guy whose name I can't remember. Over the meal it was proposed they put into production, copies of my Griffon 380, and we offered to buy 50% of their total production of this model.

On our arrival back at our shop I got a phone

Alan on his Bultaco and me on my Neval Greeves - Lincolnshire

Alan on his Neval Greeves - Lincolnshire

call from Ralling saying they had decided we had to buy from them, on a contract basis, 100% of the production of the modified 380 Griffon. We said no thanks to this, but added we would still buy 50% of their Griffon 380 production. Ralling then asked me if I would give him the Mikuni carb settings that I used on my Neval Greeves 380 so I gave him all this information, It went quiet for a couple of weeks and we had sold all our stock of Griffons so I rang Greeves to order more standard bikes but was told they couldn't sell us the standard bikes anymore as they were going to release a modified version, which would be a new model called Griffon 380 mark two. This would be a copy, it would seem, of my bike, apart from, their version would have Marzocchi leading axle front forks. The factory BSA rider, Vic Eastwood tested the new Greeves 380 mark 2 in a full page test in Motor Cycle News. Vic Eastwood's words in the article were;

'I could win a world championship round on this bike' As far as I know Greeves only put about 35 to 40 Mark 2 380 Griffon's in production as they were waiting for a shipment of magnetos for ages, and couldn't finish off their first full batch of bikes. By now they were on their last legs and after a big fire

Greeves went out of business. The two Neval Greeves that me and Alan had used were sold.

At the time that we were running the 380cc Greeves Griffons the factory was not doing any new development work on them, apart from an army contract they were trying to obtain using their standard, out of date machines. I can't think of anybody else in England who was doing any work or modifications to the Greeves bikes as we were. In 1975 and 1976 our modified Neval Greeves were out there winning races most weekends. The modifications we made to these bikes turned an out of date machine into a winner which was why the factory decided to copy our bikes, and that's a true fact not fiction, in spite of what many of the so called Greeves experts say. The factory also gave me a brand new 250cc Griffon engine and gearbox unit to develop for them which I did quite a lot of work on, getting the power up quite a bit from their standard unit, in fact it even won two races when slotted into my 380 Griffon frame. Greeves never ever asked for this 250cc engine back but at least it was some small payment for my time and work and the ideas they copied from our bikes for their new Griffon QUB 380cc Mk ll.

Around this time my mother was still living in our old house and shop in West Dock Avenue. A bunch of so called Hells Angels were squatting in the empty house next door and were causing Mum a lot of problems with their wild all night parties etcetera, the usual sort of stuff this type of imitation Hells Angels gets up to, hard men threatening an old woman, so I went down to ask them to calm it down a bit. The so called hard man of the bunch started telling me what he was going to do to me if I didn't go away. Feeling very brave with all his mates looking on he took a swing at me but unfortunately for him I just stepped sideways, and as his momentum carried him past me, a quick crack on his jaw reduced him to a heap, now sleeping on the floor. All the rest of them, seeing what had just happened to their great leader, lost interest in any further confrontation. My many years of living on Hessle Road had taught me never to back away from trouble, always attack the biggest in the gang first, sort him out and the rest will usually just disappear, and this was no exception.

Leaving them to recover their gallant leader from his sleep on the pavement, I went to make sure Mum was ok, and told her if there was any more trouble from them to ring me. About three days after this episode Mum rang to say that the low lives had wiped human excrement all over her shop window. I was at Doug Hackings in Bolton picking up some bikes, three hours away, so I rang my brother Pete and asked him if he could go and sort it out until I got back to Hull. Pete helped Mum to clean the shop windows but the so called Angels had, it seemed, gone out for the day.

This was Saturday so I thought I would leave it until Monday before going to sort them out. Anyway, Sunday morning dawned, today was our practice day at Catwick Sand Pits so me, John and Marty loaded up our bikes and off we went. Alan, Geoff and a lot of the regulars were also there and it was a good day. On our return home we found Val, Deb and Margaret (Marty's girl friend), in our front room, scared and with the curtains closed. It seems the brave, imitation Angels had been threatening women yet again. Val said they had left only 10 minutes before after sitting on their bikes in a semi circle, facing my house for about 15 minutes, revving their engines up and shouting threats at the women inside. Ok, what to do? If I call the police they will do zero, go through all the motions and achieve nothing. Val said that as they left they were shouting they would be back, and Deb said she had counted seven of them on their bikes. They must have thought they were the Magnificent Seven but they didn't look very Magnificent when I had finished with them.

I had a gut feeling that they were going to target Nevals shop later that night. It was about eight thirty and dark when I thought I heard the sound of bike engines in the next street to ours. I put my MX crash helmet on and told John and Marty to wait there while I went to check the back of Nevals shop, which was down a passage under a railway bridge. As I looked up on top of the railway embankment, a cluster of these idiots were outlined against the skyline, most wearing their very fashionable Nazi helmets. Seething with rage at the low lives who had threatened my family, I leapt up a six foot high brick wall and climbed the steep railway embankment. In the dark I managed to get right in amongst them before they realised they had an intruder in their midst. Now I really was in a blind rage and all hell broke loose. I had already downed two of them before the rest even twigged just what was going on. Never have six Hells Angels been demolished so quickly. Bodies lay everywhere.

Number seven decided to make a run for it, but in my anger, he was no match for my new found Olympian sprinting, nobody was going to threaten my family and get away with it. I grabbed number seven so hard it broke his left arm. John, Marty and the police now all arrived together. On the track was a two gallon can, full of petrol, and number seven admitted, after a slight bit of arm twisting, that they intended to fire the shop with it. Even with all the evidence the Police had, the full petrol can etc. they still threatened to charge me with assaulting the seven Hells Angels, however, the next day they said there would be no charges against me. After this the so called Hell's Angels never troubled me or my family again.

Chapter 8

The little red Russian 125 Minsk that had arrived in a batch of bikes from Cooks, and was sat in the garage behind my house, was now about to start another chapter in my business and personal life. Me and Alan went to Earls Court Motorcycle Exhibition in London. We had gone to find out what agencies were available to expand our growing empire. Satra Industrial were the importers for England for the full range of low priced Russian motorcycles. We spent about two hours on their very large stand studying the Minsk 125's they had on display, plus the 650cc Dnieper outfits and Jupiter 350cc outfits, but most of their staff seemed more interested in talking to each other and ignoring any potential customers. Getting fed up with standing around waiting for some attention I finally collared Colin Hornsby, who turned out to be the rep for our area and asked him if he had a dealer in Hull.

'Yes, Miles on Anlaby Road' he answered.

'How long have they been selling these Cossack bikes for you?' I wanted to know.

'About 9 months now'.

'And how many bikes have they sold for you in Hull? I asked. He disappeared to ask his boss this question and returned to tell me.

'4 bikes up to now.' I explained to him that we had three shops in Hull and if he would give us the agency we would guarantee to buy a minimum of 10 bikes a month from them. He looked startled and said that he would call and see us when the show had finished.

Six days after the end of the show he appeared at our Beverley Road shop to talk areas. He offered us the rights to sell in Hull only, but I declined telling him that to do the job properly, I needed from Hull to Scarborough, Scarborough to Pickering, Pickering to Doncaster and Doncaster to Grimsby. He was taken aback at the size of the area we wanted and said that he would have to check with his boss. He was back the next day with the area we wanted on a contract. All signed up we ordered 8 Minsk 125's, 4 Voskhod 175's, 2 Jupiter 350's, 1 solo and 1 outfit, 2 Dnieper 650's, 1 solo and 1 outfit, 18 bikes in total. We advertised the first week and sold 7 Minsk 125's, 3 Voskhod 175's, both the Jupiter's and both the Dnieper 650's. 14 bikes sold .

This was yet another right place, right time situation. Satra Industrial's full bike division was in the process of moving from Byfleet in Surry to Bridlington in Yorkshire where their Lada and Moskovich car divisions were based. This was ideal for us, being only 20 miles away. Over the next few months we made regular trips to Bridlington to collect bikes from their compound. We were selling around 15 Russian bikes a week now.

Cossack was Satra's brand name for all the Russian bikes they sold on the UK market. Bob Manns, the ex, six day trials and enduro rider, and Alan Kimber, ex Suzuki, were the managers of the motorcycle division at Carnaby (the industrial estate at Bridlington). I was in Bob Mann's office one day getting paperwork for the bikes I was picking up and Len Eady, the spares manager was also there. I was asked if I was interested in buying larger amounts of bikes if the price was reduced accordingly. I asked for more details, what amounts, what prices etc. and they looked at each other then Len Eady spoke up. He told me they had there, about 750 bikes which they could sell me at special prices, and there were probably another 150 or so at the Catfoss aircraft storage hangers. I spent four hours going around with them to see the bikes. Approximately 500 were Minsk 125's still in the original boxes with about 90 more out of boxes, about 210 Voskhod 175's, 350 Jupiter sidecar outfits and solo's, plus about 63 Planeta 350 Sports and Dnieper sidecar outfits and solo's.

'Why don't you buy them all Nev?' Len Eady joked.

'Why not' I replied ' OK get me a price for the lot' I said. Two days later I had a phone call from Satra asking me to go up there and meet Baccy Ornish the owner of Satra Industrial International.

I went to Bridlington to have the meeting with the boss who was quite a pleasant guy. I asked if they had a price worked out yet, but they were waiting for Len Eady who had the figures, so we passed the time talking about the weather, as you do. It was a long drag to Ornish's office but Len arrived eventually red faced and out of breath and passed a piece of paper across to his boss.

'£50,000 the lot.'

'Too much' I replied. 'Make it £45,000 and I'll have a go'

'That's plus VAT I hope' he said..

'No' I said 'That includes VAT' Shaking his head he said,

'We'll lose money on them at this rate'.

'That's no problem' I answered. 'Just claim it back as a tax loss'. Grinning like a Cheshire Cat he stuck his hand out and indicated we had a deal but I refused to shake his hand yet. I explained that two conditions would have to apply to the deal. The first was because I didn't have room to store that number of bikes they would have to stay in their present storage place, at their expense, and I would just draw off them until they were all gone, and the second was that we only had £30,000 in cash but would guarantee to pay the remaining £15,000 within 8 weeks. They agreed to these terms and noted them down.

'The full agreement will be ready to sign by 2.30 tomorrow is that OK?'

'Yes, I'll see you tomorrow'. I hurried back to the shop to excitedly tell Alan about the deal I had just done but he was less than enthusiastic.

'I don't want anything to do with it' he said quite adamantly.

'OK, its no problem, I'll buy them all myself' I told him and went home. I had already worked out that

I could just about afford the deal without Alan's involvement if necessary but at 8.30 the next morning there was a loud knocking on my front door which Val answered.

'It's Alan, he wants to speak to you.' Alan stood in the hallway with a sheepish grin on his face.

'I've given a lot of thought to the Satra deal and if you're prepared to take a chance on them, then so am I.' Went back to Satra that afternoon and signed the agreement.

For the next few weeks we worked flat out collecting bikes from Bridlington and Catfoss and selling them. In just 9 weeks we were able to pay the £15,000 cash we still owed Satra from sales, and within 8 months we had our original £45,000 investment back, and we still had approximately 425 bikes left in stock, all now fully paid for. I went to see Baccy Ornish to give him the cheque for the £15,000. He seemed very pleased with it, but had another proposition for me.

'Nev, before you go, tell me, would you be interested in a full time job working at Satra? We need someone like you to run our motorcycle division here at Bridlington.'

'What would be involved?' I asked out of

curiosity.

'Well, you would run the division as if it was your own. Pay would be £25,000 a year to start, plus a new four bed roomed house in Bridlington and a top of the range Lada as a company car and a good pension.' I thought for a few minutes then asked.

'Who would I be accountable to?'

'Me' he said .

'Sorry, I'm not interested. I like being my own boss, if I make a mistake it's my business, my fault. If I made a mistake in your business then I would have to explain myself to you.' He was disappointed but accepted what I was saying, he recognised something in me that was unfortunately missing from his own staff. I left his office, never ever to see him again.

When I told Alan about the conversation with Ornish he said I was an idiot and should have taken the job.

'Could you really see me working for Ornish?' I asked him. He gave it about 5 seconds thought then said.

'NO'.

Within a couple of months of this we had a visit from a delegation of officials from the Russian Trade

Delegation in London, headed by Mr Kolosov, Mr Safonov and Mr Popov. They asked us if we would be interested in taking over, as the official importers for England, all the Russian bikes sold by Avtoexport, the worldwide selling agents in Moscow, who acted for all the Russian motorcycle producing factories. Also with the delegation was Anatol Miychenko who was to become my chief factory technician and a life long personal friend. Mr Kolosov asked if he could ask me a personal question I said.

'Yes, of course.' He then said.

'Satra Motors is a very big, multi million dollar, world wide company as you know, so how is it that you can sell large numbers of our Russian motorcycles and they can't?'

'Its very simple' I said ' We know our job better than they do. First we don't just sell the bikes in the standard condition as Satra tried, we have a list of modifications we make to each model before we sell it. Take the Minsk for example, the factory deliberately designed the front brake to work without too much power because in the snow in Russia a too powerful front brake would cause the front of the bike to slip away, causing a crash. For our English roads we need a strong front brake so we make the front operating brake arm longer, for more leverage, and change the front brake cable for an English manufactured one that doesn't compress when it's pulled on. This simple modification gives the bike a good front brake. We also change the rear lamp which is too dim for the UK, and each bike is given a 53 point pre delivery inspection before it goes out on a one mile test run. This way we know everything is working OK when it leaves us to go to the customer, and this same system is applied to all the Russian bikes we sell.'

'Would you be interested in visiting our factories in Russia to show them the modifications and P.D.I. inspections you do here, as this would help us to improve our bikes for other markets in the world?' Kolosov asked. Alan looked at me and I looked at him, no words were spoken, or needed to be, but his thoughts were exactly the same as mine; Go to Russia, you must be bl…dy joking, but we said we would think about it for the future.

'We would like you to attend a meeting at our Trade Delegation in Highgate, London where our boss, Mr Zamyatin would like to meet you to propose some mutual business interests?' So a date was set up to meet the number one, Mr Zamyatin a week or so later. We timed it to coincide with me and Derek Lockwood delivering Neval Minsk 125 bikes to customers in that area.

We arrived late at about 7.30 in the evening in a Datsun Pickup pulling a car trailer, which we had just used to deliver 14 Neval 125 cc. We were met at the entrance gate to the Delegation buildings by Anatol who directed us into the Delegation's car park.

The Datsun Pickup and car trailer didn't look right parked amongst the Mercedes, Audi, Jaguars and BMW's etc. What we were not aware of, was this was an official Trade Delegation, export party we had arrived at. Anatol didn't look impressed by the way me and Derek were dressed. I explained we had been out delivering Russian bikes to customers in London so we were not dressed for a business party.

He called a lift which took us up 3 floors to his Delegation accommodation. He then proceeded to find us some more appropriate clothes to wear. Looking a bit smarter, we were ushered into the party accompanied by Anatol and introduced to the top guy Mr Zamyatin, who chastised us for being late. Anatol explained to me that he dare not tell him we had been out delivering bikes all day to our customers.

This is where I first developed an interest in Russian Vodka, and the food wasn't bad either. Zamyatin had a very abrupt nature and called a spade a spade, a bit similar to me, so we got on very well. He was very insistent that we visit Russia and help their factories to improve the machines for selling in the western world. He even offered to lay on a private plane, at the Delegation's expense. Suddenly we felt like visiting royalty, even so, visiting royalty or not, the thought of going to Russia, I will admit, frightened me to death, and I know Alan felt exactly the same. People would say to us.

'You'll never come back if you go' or the other favourite was,

'They'll brainwash you.'

Anatol found us a room to stay for the night, as due to too much vodka we were in no fit state to drive, but after a good nights sleep and with a clear head we set off back home. It had been a good evening at the Trade Delegation party and I made quite a few, good, British business contacts there.

The Datsun pickups that we used were bought new from D C Cooks for £1000 each, a yellow one and a blue one. The yellow one had 194,000 miles on the clock when we sold it, from delivering bikes all over the UK but the blue one had only 63,000 as it had spent half its life off the road, having had two major crashes and many breakdowns. It just shows that no two vehicles are ever the same even from brand new.

It got busier and busier at the Beverley Road shop so now we just used the De Grey Street shop for storage. We regularly advertised in MCN, the weekly motorcycle paper, which sold our bikes, mainly Dnieper 650's and Jupiter 350's, solo and sidecar trim, but we never sold many Neval 125's, (our brand name for the Minsks), through this type of M/C magazine. We sold a lot in our local area of Hull and the surrounding district, in fact at 5 p.m. every evening it was like a red tide swarming along Beverley Road. You couldn't go anywhere in Hull without seeing Neval 125's everywhere.

I once went to Queens Gardens Police Station, the main police station in Hull, to collect a BSA C15 they had recovered for us and I couldn't believe my eyes when I counted in the parking area 11 Neval 125's and 4 Voskhod 175's, even the police officers were buying and using our bikes for cheap to run, get to work, transport.

To increase sales of the Neval 125's we paid £500 for a series of 10 adverts on Yorkshire TV and we sold about 17 Neval 125's from it. Good, but not good enough, we needed advertising that would reach the main market, the ride to work man who wanted cheap transport simply to get to work and back. Sat on our shop counter one day was a copy of The Daily Mirror which somebody had left behind and suddenly the penny dropped. Who reads the Daily Mirror six days a week, yes, got it in one, working men. I rang the advertising department of the Mirror on the Tuesday and placed an advert to appear in the Thursday morning edition, and spent the days between wondering what sort of response we would get.

At 9am on Thursday, the phone was ringing as I unlocked the shop door, and it rang continually all day, and I mean all day. That first ad in the Mirror produced 57 sales by the end of the first day. Selling at only £179 on the road with free delivery anywhere in England and a full guarantee we had found the Holy Grail of advertising for these cheap, ride to work bikes. We sold, over the next week, an additional 32 bikes, 89 Neval 125's sold in less than one week.

What we had also proved was that there was still a big market for low priced, simple motorcycles, just like my Dad had proved 28 years earlier with the brand new 50cc scooters he bought at the Auction on Hull docks and sold at low prices.

The Daily Mirror phenomenon continued week after week. Our best week from the Mirror ad was 119 bikes. In late October 1977, with 4 inches of snow on the ground, we lined up all the bikes we had sold that week along the street before they were loaded and delivered. What an impressive sight it was. We took a photo which we used in our future adverts for a long time. There was one particular month in 1977 when Russian motorcycle sales, by Nevals in East Yorkshire took nearly 46% of the total registered bike sales.

NEV, NOBODY LIKES TO SEE OTHERS BEING SUCCESSFUL PARTICULARLY WHEN IT AIN'T HAPPENING TO THEM.
QUOTE FROM BILL BROWN WULFSPORT CUMBRIA.

Nev Mason saying
1977
Opportunities will always pass you by in life unless you learn to recognise them

Chapter 9

We would have to give some serious thought to going to the factories in Russia if we wanted to continue to expand the business, so we finally telephoned Anatol and told him we would make the trip. Resigning myself to death, or at least never to return, me and Alan went to London's Heathrow airport and climbed aboard a huge Russian plane along with Anatol, Mr Kolosov and some other Russian guys who I didn't know. When the plane arrived at Moscow airport it was dark outside and it made two abortive attempts at landing on the frozen, snow covered runway. Even the Russians were beginning to look worried but thankfully on the third attempt it landed successfully. I think both me and Alan must have aged about 10 years but eventually we were ushered through customs and out of the airport to waiting cars.

We were driven to a big hotel, and I mean huge, where we stayed that night and at nine o'clock the next morning Mr Kolosov knocked on our door and entered, followed by a waiter with a fully laden breakfast trolley. There was enough food on the trolley to feed an army. At about 10.30 he informed us that we had to go back to the airport to fly to Minsk, so breakfast over and a quick wash and brush up and we were back in the cars and whisked off to catch our next plane.

For the first time it was becoming obvious to us just how powerful these Russian guys were in their own country. As the cars rushed us to the airport all other vehicles were ushered out of the way and at the airport the cars drove round the main building and parked up next to a twin winged biplane that looked like a left over from World War One. We were urged by Anatol to get on board as the pilot wanted to get going. It carried four passengers and I asked where Mr Kolosov was, as he was not on board with us and the door was now shut. I asked Alan if he had noticed the tyres and looking out of the window he went a whiter shade of pale. The canvas was showing on both the tyres. Again I asked Anatol why Kolosov was not with us.

'Perhaps he had more sense than us' he said with a grin 'he told me he had urgent business to sort out at his office and he would join us in Minsk tomorrow.' The planes engine burst into life and as we started to taxi to the take off point I noticed that the propeller was out of balance and the vibration through the plane was intense.

'This must be the resigning myself to death bit' I thought. The plane flew all the way to Minsk no more than 300 feet above the ground, no kidding and my, was I glad when it finally landed at Minsk airport.

We were greeted by a large group of people from the factory. Anatol explained that many of them had never met anyone from England before and joked that maybe they wanted to see if we had two arms and two legs like them. It was Saturday and we were taken to the Planeta Hotel which was a very modern looking place, and given a room on the seventh floor. A restaurant meal had been arranged by the factory for us and before eating we were introduced to Mr Klenikski, the Minsk factory director who spoke no English.

Russian hospitality is out of this world and we had a very pleasant evening, but one of the problems when visiting and dealing in Russia, is the constant making of toasts, which are accompanied by a tot of high octane vodka, drunk in one swig. Anatol told me that after every eight toasts or so I should go to the toilets and make myself sick to get rid of it all, to avoid becoming too drunk, but this method also gets rid of all the food as well. That seemed a waste.

The factory normally doesn't work on a Sunday but Mr Klenikski turned the factory in so we could see it working. The sheer size of the place was mind blowing. They made everything, even the bike's frame tubing was made on site from flat steel. A full tour of the plant followed and we saw our next order of bikes being prepared for shipment to us, complete with all the modifications we had shown them were needed for our UK market, along with the new electronic ignition, new carburettor and new type tyres which they were now fitting for us. All very impressive. We went back to the Planeta Hotel after thanking them for the tour.

The elusive Mr Kolosov turned up at about nine o'clock that night and soon after Alan jokingly asked if there were any saunas open at this time on a Sunday. Mr Kolosov said he would check and ten minutes later re-appeared and collected us all up to go to the main baths in Minsk. Again this shows the power these people in high places had, because he had got this big swimming complex to open on a Sunday night just for us. The cars which seemed to be on permanent standby carried us to the complex and inside, laid out in a large side room was a table groaning with food and drink. The Minsk factory director, Mr Klenikski was also

Top: Mine and Alan's 1st visit to the Minsk Plant
Bottom: Can you spot the KGB guy?

Top: 1st Minsk Plant visit
Bottom: 1st Dnieper Plant visit

there. I had never learned to swim properly so a qualified coach was brought in at 11.30 at night, to teach me how to swim confidently and at around 3 o'clock in the morning we went back to the hotel to rest. We just seemed to get off to sleep when there was a knock on the door urging us to get up.

'P..s off we need some sleep.' But Anatol was insistent. We had another plane to catch to take us to Kiev for another factory visit. This was all starting to get a bit too much for me and Alan, and too tired to rush, we kept the plane waiting while we leisurely got ready. They were obviously not used to this type of go slow.

We were glad to see, when we finally got to the airport, that the plane was a normal large airliner. It sat, fully loaded, waiting for us to arrive and we were embarrassed to see on entering, just our four places were left un-occupied. We sat down and then were surprised to see other passengers getting on, I counted 16 extra people, who were all now stood in the centre aisle holding on to the seat backs. I really didn't think the plane was going to get off the ground with all this extra weight on board, but it did, eventually. We landed with a very heavy thump at Kiev airport in the Ukraine and even Kolosov looked relieved.

We went straight to the hotel to catch up on some sleep. The next day we were driven out of Kiev, where the factory was situated, into the countryside, and after about 10 miles the 4 x 4, UAZ van, which had windows and seats fitted in it, turned off into the woods. Me and Alan looked at each other not knowing what to think, but we cleared the woods, and entered a very large moto cross sports complex. MX sidecar outfits and solo bikes were going round on two different tracks. The factory, knowing of our interest in moto cross had organised a MX practice day in our honour. Suddenly this wasn't so frightening anymore. They may speak a different language, but these idiots had just the same interest as me and Alan, leaping around on off road motorcycles.

Anatol asked us if we wanted to have a ride round the track on one of the bikes, so putting on a set of leathers over my normal clothes, I was given a 750 flat twin MX outfit, plus a very brave passenger, to try it out. Anatol borrowed this volunteer passenger from another outfit for me. This bike was seriously fast and handled very well, the main problem was that the side car was fitted on the right hand side, as opposed to the

English left hand side, but I had some good fun for about 10 laps then came in for a rest. I thanked the passenger, Sasha, for his expert assistance. Anatol also borrowed for me a CZ 250 MX bike and I had about 15 minutes riding this. Alan and I really enjoyed this unexpected day.

Mr Kolosov felt he had to give a party political speech to the assembled crowd about how co-operation with us would help to improve the bikes. Me and Alan stood there looking embarrassed until he had finished his speech then we shook hands with as many people as possible and were driven back to the hotel at Kiev.

The next day was very interesting. The factory had recently been extended to double its previous size and the main assembly line was three quarters of a kilo metre long. Our tour of the factory took about five hours including visiting the Factory's MX team workshop and the road race team workshop, where there were some special outfits powered by four cylinder, water cooled, two stroke, flat four engines which were only allowed to be raced in Russia, we were told by Anatol, and a very special Military side car division that had a full fleet of Khaki coloured test outfits.

A meeting was arranged by Anatol, as this was the factory he worked for. There was a long table in the directors office around which sat 24 factory heads of various departments. Talks went well until a guy called Ivan who ran the experimental department said he didn't want to co-operate with us.

'How can they know what is best for us to do' he said quite sharply. 'I don't see why we have to co-operate with an English company at all'. It's at moments like this that you really have to be there to get the full impact. Anatol gave me a nudge and a wink and said quietly.

'Watch this'. He reached into his inside jacket pocket and pulled out a small red book. He didn't say a word, didn't need to, just put the book onto the table in front of himself. A deathly hush descended around the table and Ivan totally lost interest in what he had been saying and just sat down. Still without saying a word Anatol picked up the book and put it back in his pocket. This guy Ivan eventually became one of our best allies in the factory for all future modifications we were to make. He also made sure that all the major components on our future Dnieper's would have the

Russian Red Star Military Cross stamped on them, as this was the sign of quality components. The military wouldn't accept bad components for their bikes so they made sure they were all made and stamped to the high standards they set for the factory.

With a full list of modifications agreed on the MT10 36 sidecar outfits, the meeting was over. It was about 10.30 in the evening and time to catch our return flight to Moscow but for some unknown reason I refused point blank to travel on the pre-arranged plane. I just couldn't face this flight I don't know why but no amount of persuasion could have got me on to it. I insisted we return to Moscow by train. Kolosov started to loose the plot and get angry, insisting that we go to the airport or we would miss the flight, but I also insisted that I was not going to fly, and was adamant that I was going to travel by one of the trains that run 24 hours to Moscow, and if not by train I would get a taxi back. Realizing how serious I was Anatol had slipped out, and in ten minutes had organised the return trip by over night train.

Alan was a bit inebriated to say the least but I was ok, as I had been going to the toilet every couple of hours, as previously instructed by Anatol, to make myself sick. We all boarded the train with most of the objections now forgotten and were directed to our sleeping compartments. Suddenly Alan decided to be sick. What a mess, it was everywhere, he even managed to get it all over the shiny new leather brief case that the factory had presented to me at the meeting. I was moved to the next compartment while Anatol spent a good two hours cleaning everything up, including Alan and my new brief case, we joked about this for many years.

A steady speed throughout the night saw us arrive at Moscow Central Station and we were met on the platform by Oleg, a guy from Avtoexport's office. All the Russians went into a huddle in the middle of the platform with much 'ooing' and 'ahing.'

'Now what's gone wrong' I thought. Anatol came back over to us with a strange look on his face.

'Nev, we have just heard that the plane we should have all been on last night crashed. How... did you know it was going to crash?'

'I didn't know it would crash' I said 'all I knew was that if I had been offered a million pounds I would not have got on that plane.' After this incident they were all convinced that I was a visionary and could see into the future.

Val had seen the report on the news on TV about the plane crash and knew this was the plane we should have been on. I got Anatol to book a telephone call to her, as in those days, in Russia you had to book all outside calls at least two hours ahead, but when I did get through she was very relieved to know me and Alan were both still alive and well.

Back at the headquarters of Avtoexport we were having a round the table discussion of the events of the past few days. During a break Alan went off to the toilet and Anatol left to organise a meal. The mysterious Oleg came over to me and asked if he could have a quick word with me. He said.

'Mr Mason, would you have any interest in looking after our interests in England?' Being a bit thick it took me a while to cotton on to what he was asking.

'What, do you mean spy?'

'Well yes, I suppose that's what I'm asking.'

'No' I said 'my total interests in life are my family, my MX and my passion for motorcycles. I am willing to help your factories improve their bikes and that's all.'

'OK Mr Mason, thank you for your very frank answer, but I had to ask you this question, it's part of my job.'

The next day we flew back to England and I had been at home for no more than an hour when there was a knock on my front door. Val answered the door to two well dressed men who asked for me by name. Val called to me in the kitchen, where I was enjoying a cup of tea, that I was wanted at the door. I was asked to confirm my name, which I did, then, showing me their ID, I was told they were from a special department in London. The older one said that they understood I had just returned from a trip to Russia.

'Yes, I got back about an hour ago.' I said. They asked me would I accompany them to the police station as they had some questions they wanted to ask about my visit so I told Val that I had to go out with these guys to a meeting and left with them. I was taken to a room at the rear of the Hull Central Police Station where one other man was already waiting and I was asked to sit down. The questions started with

'What do you think to it in Russia?' So I explained that at first I didn't want to go there as my only experience of what it would be like was from TV and films, but was glad that I had finally made the trip as it was nothing like I had expected it to be. All the people that we had met, including workers at the factories, were all OK, and it was much better than I had feared it would be. They then asked if I had seen any military tanks on my visit.

'No, I don't remember seeing any tanks at all but then I wasn't looking for tanks, I went looking for anything to do with motorcycles, not tanks.'

'So what were your overall impressions of Russia?' I told them

'I found that all the people we met were interested in just the same things as us. They thought a lot about how they could improve life for their families, how they could buy a better car or a bigger apartment, they were only interested in the same things we are all interested in, improving their lives.' I explained 'I even discovered that there were the same sort of idiots in Russia as in England with the same obsessions for moto cross that I have. One of the guys asked if there was much for customers to buy in the shops. I told him.

'Most of the shops I saw had goods in the windows on display, but not as much as UK shops have on display, but if you are that interested why don't you just buy a plane ticket and go and have a look for yourself?' This didn't seem to go down too well at all, and I was then asked.

'During your visit, Mr Mason, did anyone ask you if you would be interested in helping them with their observations'

'You mean spy?' I said

'Yes'

'As a matter of fact I was asked if I would spy for them but I told them I was not interested at all. My only interest is in helping them to develop their motorcycles.' The older guy smiled and said.

'Yes, we know that you were asked' I was speechless. Was the secretive Oleg a UK double agent? It was a good job I had not shown any interest in his proposition. Before leaving I said to them.

'I hope you are not going to ask me to spy for you lot, because the answer's just the same as I gave to the Russians. I really am not interested.'

'Mr Mason we wouldn't dream of asking you such a question, if you are not interested then you are not interested.' I was then taken home.

Chapter 10

We had our first international show at Earls Court, London where we exhibited our full range of modified Neval bikes. It was a good show for us and we took a lot of orders. Mr Safonov from the Trade Delegation visited to see how things were going and he seemed pleased with the stand and the new bikes. Before he left he presented us with 8 cases of Stolichnaya Vodka, 6 bottles to a case, which we shared around the other stands near us and by about 4 o'clock in the afternoon there were inebriated bodies lolling everywhere on the stands around us. It's strong stuff, Russian vodka. At least 5 members of the motorcycle press had propped themselves on our stand, and were now on a trip to another planet. The next day the show press secretary asked us not to bring anymore vodka to the stand, but many people still remember that day, or don't, depending on how much they'd had to drink .

We attended most of the big exhibitions with our new range, Birmingham, Belle Vue, Manchester etc, and started to put together a UK dealer network. On the MX front, we brought in the first Yamaha XT500 trail bikes to convert to MX trim. I used one and Alan had one and Geoff Stokes bought the third one from us to convert. The first meeting with all three of us on the converted XT500's was at Ripon. Alan Clews, boss of CCM was there with his full team of CCM works riders, Bob Wright, Norman Barrow and Andy Ainsworth. In the first race me, Alan and Geoff literally smoked all the works CCMs to the first corner on power, and all three Neval Yamahas ran in the top six all day. I remember saying to Clews, after the meeting,

'Alan, what you need are some of these converted Yamaha XT trail bikes to race' He didn't seem to be at all amused and Doug Hacking jokingly cautioned him not to be so serious. I ran my XT 500 for over a year without any problems at all and Alan had no mechanical problems with his bike either, but Geoff had some engine and gearbox problems with his bike.

We also now took on the agency for the Italian Benelli 750cc, 650cc, 250cc and 125cc bikes. They were plagued with electrical problems and within less than a year we dropped them as they were so much trouble. Mechanical problems can be relatively easy to solve but electrical work on bikes can be a nightmare. We weren't alone having electrical problems on Italian bikes.

We had a big shipment of Neval Dnieper, 650 MT10 36 military outfits arrive. Ten were sold to Coburn and Hughes, the Ducati and Guzzi importers for the UK. They had sold them on to a German company they dealt with. I delivered them to their Luton depot with John, my son, who was now starting to take an interest in the business. We arrived and unloaded all the outfits and was paid for them. I noticed about 11 Ducatti's and 4 Guzzi's in the workshop having work done to them. I wandered over and got talking to the workshop foreman who confirmed that most of these bikes were having warranty work done, for either electrical or mechanical faults. I must have looked surprised to him, about all this remedial work, but he said as if to redress the balance.

'I bet you have even more problems with your Russian bikes.'

'Honestly, you couldn't be more wrong.' I answered genuinely. 'Our warranty rate is about 2% a month on average on all our bikes. If I had all this to contend with,' I gestured to his workshop, 'I would retire.'

In all the years we ran Nevals it sold thousands

of bikes, and I do mean thousands, and I only ever had one court case with a customer who ran his new 50cc two stroke on neat petrol, no oil in it, and destroyed the engine and then tried to blame the bike. I had the engine stripped by an independent engineer who reported to the court that there was no sign of there being any oil at all inside the engine. Nevals won the case. My way of thinking is that if a customer has a problem, sort it out for him or offer him his money back. It really isn't worth arguing about.

A customer called Mr Renner bought a new Neval 125 and for three weeks we had to go to his house almost every day to get it started for him as he kept flooding the engine. He couldn't see that it was his fault and was getting upset. We were also getting upset, so I gave him his money back. We gave the bike a full check over and put it back into stock and sold it again the next day. Now, with a different owner, the same bike gave no more problems and about 12 years later I was in a restaurant in Hull having lunch with an old friend when there was a tap on my shoulder and Dave Lockhart, the guy who bought the Renner bike said 'Hey up Nev, I haven't seen you for a long time.' We got talking and he said he still had the little Neval

125 he bought from us in 1978 and it now had 28,600 km on the clock and was still going strong. I find it fascinating that the first owner had loads of problems but the second owner ran the same bike for 12 years problem free. There's now't as strange as folk.

We had a show coming up in Birmingham and me and Anatol took the bikes for exhibit in a Transit, box van that Nevals had just bought. The engine was only 1600 cc and it made hard work of pulling the large alloy body, fitted with a roll up rear door. Going into the wind it had a top speed of about 45 mph but with the wind behind it, it would do 80 mph. On this day we were going into the wind.

Anatol was very talkative on this trip telling me how he was put into an orphanage in Kiev when he was five years old because his parents had both died. He was quite open about being a member of the Communist Party and explained that the only way you progressed in Russia was if you were a card carrying member. He was taken out of the orphanage by the KGB when he was 12 years old and from that age until he was 22 was taught in a special academy, by KGB instructors, whose job it was to indoctrinate his mind against the western world. He was now about 40, and he said he was fully trained before he was finally allowed to leave the USSR on missions. He told me that on his first outside trip he was sent to Ethiopia.

'What did you do there?' I asked him.

'I was supposed to spy and report back every week on what there was or what was happening in Ethiopia' he said.

'To spy on them' I said sounding surprised. 'Spy on what?' Laughing he said

'What's that word you say in Yorkshire Nev? Nowt. Absolutely nowt. There's nothing there to spy on' He had a good dry sense of humour. He went on to say that when he was posted to Germany, then later to England, as an Avtoexport factory representative it made him totally rethink everything he had been painstakingly taught by the KGB, about how bad the western world really was.

'What a total waste of ten years of my life' he said 'by all those bloody KGB people.' He freely admitted that he used the Communist system in Russia to improve his and his family's lifestyle, get a bigger flat, a better car and many perks in life you could not get otherwise.

I got on very well with Anatol as we had a

common interest, motorcycles. It seemed that part of his KGB training was to get involved in sport and he chose motorcycle ice speedway and moto cross. He said that he had been the ice racing champion twice, a fact that was confirmed when me and Val visited his home and factory in Kiev, many years later, and he showed us his collection of the trophies he had won, both in ice racing and moto cross.

The conversation made for an interesting journey but we eventually arrived at the show, unloaded the bikes and started to set up our stand. We were just about finished when some idiots arrived and said that they had the contract with the organisers of the show and they, and only they, were permitted to assemble all the stands in the entire show. The show Gestapo eventually arrived and demanded we disassemble everything. It was obviously a point we were not going to win so we took it all apart and then sat on a couple of chairs and watched them while they assembled it all up again. Anatol thought it was hilarious,

'Its just like being in Russia' he joked.

It was a good show for our new model Neval 125 Electronic, with its smart new chrome mudguards and finished in a new, lighter shade of a special, Italian red paint. And with its new seat, new graphics, new carb and electronic ignition, it was now well updated and even had ceramic clutch plates instead of cork. There was a lot of interest in it from both dealers and the general public.

Which Bike magazine had just tested the new model Neval 125 and rated it better than the Suzuki A 100 they had tested it against. The Neval was faster, handled better, had superior brakes, plus quicker acceleration. A better all round bike than the Suzuki they said and it was also £75 cheaper to buy. It was good to know that all our work to improve the bikes specification for the UK market had been noticed by the test rider and editor of Which Bike, Mark Williams.

On the journey back from the show I asked Anatol if he could get the Minsk factory to paint 50% of the next shipment of Minsk in blue instead of red,

'That's 50% red and the other 50% all blue.' I said. This was when I first discovered that when dealing with foreign factories you have to make sure everything is explained in great detail and also all requirements put down in writing.

Anatol, as requested asked the factory to make

the next shipment; 100 in red as usual and 100 blue. Two months later the shipment of 200 bikes arrived and we were all eager to see the Neval 125 in its new blue colour. The first box was opened and me, Alan, Anatol and all the Neval's staff in the vicinity gasped in amazement. The request for 100 bikes to be all in blue had been taken quite literally, everything on the bike was now finished in a really nice bright blue, and I mean everything. Only the tyres were still black. The tank, seat, wheels, frame, even our prized new type chrome mudguards were now blue. I can imagine, at the factory the production people asking each other why do these English fools want the bikes all blue. We asked for blue bikes, we got blue bikes.

After this experience any future changes that were to be made, we explained in full, listing which parts should be in chrome, which in black, and so on. The all blue bikes in this shipment were offered for £25 less than the standard red and chrome ones and after two weeks it became obvious that blue was starting to out sell red. It's amazing what £25 discount can do.

We now had a full time technician from the Minsk factory, Vladimir Zebruski, aged about 45, who again had a good sense of humour. Relations were a lot better with the Minsk factory, as now we had direct communication through one of their own employees. Vlad, as we called him stayed with us for about two years and I was sad to see him go when he eventually returned to Minsk. He used to spend hours playing a ping pong, tennis game, on our television, that was all the rage at the time. He also used to love going to moto cross meetings with my family and acting as chief mechanic for me or John. Vlad was yet another guy from Russia who not only worked with us but was very open about his country's misplaced politics towards the western world. He and Anatol would have very long talks on this topic. They both said that the people and life in England were nothing like the images portrayed in Russia .

Vladimir was replaced by Ivor, a miserable, sullen type, about 60 years old who did nothing, and knew as much about motorcycles as my dogs (nothing). Why the factory sent him I don't really know, maybe they didn't know either.

Around this time we sold our Twowheels shop to Iain Lomax and Dave Johnson, two of our employees who wanted to start up on their own. It still gave Nevals an outlet for our bikes on the other side of town and they took over distribution of the Voskhod 175 for us, delivering them all over the UK. To do the deal we took Dave Johnson's mother's house in Hessle, in part exchange against our Calvert lane shop, and she was to live in the accommodation behind the shop. We also sold our shop in De Grey Street as we no longer needed it for storage because we had acquired a very large warehouse in Wincomlee, which was big enough to store several hundred bikes and spare parts. We sold the De Grey Street shop to Mick Richie, a great friend who ran Temple Supplies, a business which dealt in new and second hand motorcycle spares, and he operated from there for many years.

Around this period John my son started to show a big interest in MX. Up until now I had built him bikes to ride and his last bike, built by me, was a Honda CB 100 which was converted to MX specification. In three schoolboy meetings he had achieved good results riding amongst older riders on proper Japanese motocross bikes so I now converted a Yamaha RS100 road bike to racing spec for him. For about a year he was amongst the top lads for his age on this bike and had many wins. He even won the 125 National Grass Track championship at Beeford on it.

As he now had a keen interest in racing I finally relented and bought him a new Yamaha YZ100. In this class he had many wins, and later, when he was 12, I part exchanged the YZ100 for a YZ125 for him. I was finding it more interesting taking him to MX meetings than riding myself. It was on this bike, that he beat me for the first time during a practice session at Fimber. Going down a long steep hill he came flying past me but on the bottom corner I cut back inside and passed him back, only to find going back up the hill he came flying past me again and disappeared into the distance. I suddenly realised that now, aged 38, I had reached my sell by date as far as racing was concerned, so his racing now took priority over mine.

I was starting to steer the shop empire towards the dealer wholesale market, leaving Twowheels to concentrate on the retail side. Within a year we had 36 dealers covering all of the UK, and four distributors so a deal was done, again with Iain Lomax and Dave Johnson, to take the Calvert Lane shop we had sold them back in part exchange against our Beverley Road shop. When this transaction was finalised we then sold the Calvert Lane shop to a local plumbing firm and Iain and Dave transferred the Twowheels name to the

Beverley Road shop.

Things were changing. I had bought my previously rented house in De Grey Street plus the house on either side of it, but now fancied a move to the countryside in Lincolnshire, so I bought a three bed roomed bungalow with one acre of land at Barrow Haven, on the banks of the River Humber, and a former Chapel, which sat on one and a half acres of land, at New Holland about a mile from my new home. I have been very lucky to never have, or needed a mortgage in my life. The cash from selling the three houses in De Grey Street paid for the bungalow and the Chapel in Lincolnshire, and every house after that, when sold, paid for the next one.

Anecdote

Some highlights for me, of my scrambling days, were at age seventeen, riding my ex-Dave Curtis 500cc Matchless G80CS which I had bought from John Avery's. The first time out on it, at a big meeting at Cadwell Park, I nearly won the ten lap race. Dave Bickers passed me on the last but one lap but I had the satisfaction of beating John Draper the works BSA rider plus a whole lot of the other top names in the game. At a big meeting in Derbyshire my Matchless refused to start so I borrowed brother Pete's BSA Gold Star for the first race of the day which I won despite the slightly foggy conditions. Again I beat many of the top riders of the time which was not bad considering I had never ridden this track before, not even in practice, because my Matchless had broken down with a duff condenser in the magneto at the start of the practice session. The rest of the meeting was cancelled when thick fog descended. At a BBC TV Grandstand meeting at Ripon the same year I got the lead in the first race and beat the best riders in England to and around the first corner, but at the Ripon track there is a very large forty foot gap between two hills and being young and daft I jumped right across it at high speed. When I hit the other side the landing was so hard that the bike's frame snapped on the front down tube and the rest of my day was spent watching and nursing the area I'd hurt the most on impact, with the petrol tank between my legs. **I have many more memories from the many years I rode in scrambles but those above I remember very well.**

Top: Our Shipyard cottages after modifying them
Bottom: Our three houses in De Grey Street

Top: Family group at John and Ellen's wedding
Bottom: Woodbine Farm - Is that Rose in the background?

Chapter 11

Living in the countryside in Lincolnshire was a big jump from living in a street in Hull. This was freedom, I could walk out of my door and climb on my bike. I bought two new 1979 Maico 440's, one for me and one for John, from Bill Brown and living here we could ride for miles and miles unhindered in either direction. My dogs loved the place and luckily so did the wife and Debbie. Nevals Russian business was now operated from a large aircraft hanger on Elsham airfield. Sales and workshops were based there and the spare parts division for all the Russian bikes was operated from the chapel at New Holland. We took on a local lady, Chris Koop as a book keeper, who once again, became a lifelong family friend.

We now concentrated at Elsham on selling Dnieper 650cc Military sidecar outfits and distributing the 125cc Nevals to our dealer network and distributors, although these bikes were also still sold in Hull by Twowheels, at our old Beverley Road premises.

We used to have a couple of test outfits based at Elsham, a 750cc Dnieper MT12, two wheel drive, and a 650cc Dnieper MT10. We had a large test track in the disused chalk pit next to the airfield where customers were shown the capabilities of these outfits off road. I used to really enjoy taking customers out for test rides around the chalk quarry and I can't think of anybody who was not impressed by just where these outfits would go.

Roger Willis, the well known journalist, was given a demonstration by me and John around the quarry, showing just what the 750cc side valve twin wheel drive Dnieper could achieve off road. Sitting him in the military sidecar we spent over an hour driving around the quarry terrifying him. John showed him how the outfit was capable of a long wheelie, and for over a quarter of a mile Willis desperately clung onto the hand rails on the military sidecar body. Impressed, I'd say he was. He wrote a six page article in a motorcycle magazine, praising the outfit and saying it was the best fun he'd had in years. For many years, when I or John met him at shows and exhibitions he ranted on about what a great day it had been. It was something he said he would remember for the rest of his life.

Anatol was now relocated across to Lincolnshire

Top: 750 Dnieper MT12 twin wheel drive
Bottom: 750 Dnieper MX outfit sent by Anatol

Top: Dnieper MT14 - Police model
Bottom: Minsk 125 Sports 16hp we developed

and we found a nearly new, 4 bed roomed house for him at Grasby near Caister, at a rent of £200 per month, which the Trade Delegation paid. I also bought him a Jaguar XJ6 to run, just to sicken off his colleagues at the Trade Delegation in London as they all ran Ladas, although admittedly, they were top of the range Ladas. Anatol was a registered alien in the UK as a Russian representative and had to notify every journey he made, and the route he would take every day at Bigby Police Station. He was under 24 hour surveillance by MI6, but he said it was the same for every Russian working as a technician in the UK. I asked him how many Russian technicians there were in the UK at that time and he said he thought there were many thousands of them, attached to English companies. Even Howarth Timber in New Holland, the company that imported Russian timber had 7 Russians attached to their firm, and all were followed 24 hours a day. Just think how much employment they were generating in the UK for us.

Anatol now had Neala his wife and Leanna his youngest daughter living with him at the house in Grasby and only three weeks after their arrival, Neala was taken seriously ill during the night and had to go to Scunthorpe hospital by ambulance, but Anatol was unable to go with her as he had not given the police prior notice of this happening so he had to wait until the next day to fill in the relevant forms at the police station before being allowed to go and visit her. Fortunately she recovered OK, but I do remember thinking, where was the compassion from the police, there was none. Why couldn't an exception have been made so he could have been with her at the hospital when she needed him, but Anatol was resigned to this type of treatment.

When we were at the Dnieper factory they had shown us a very modern looking 650cc, electric start twin, they had built 4 years previously, which was scheduled to go into production in 1983. It was called the MT14 and eventually we managed to persuade the factory to send it across to us to exhibit at the coming Earls Court Show where we got a very good reception for it. We were now bringing in about 250 Dnieper outfits, 50 Dnieper solos and around 750 Minsks a year. They paid quite well, We had also started to ship Dnieper outfits to the USA, and for the next two years we continued to expand our wholesale and dealer network from our works at Elsham airfield.

One of the major reasons we didn't have much mechanical trouble with the Dnieper's we imported from the Kiev factory was because all the major components in the engine, gearbox and rear differentials were stamped with the military red star emblem. This meant they were top grade, and it was a guarantee of the quality. Geoff Stokes was riding a Norton Wasp outfit in the British sidecar MX Championships and he was doing quite well, so we took a standard road Dnieper 650cc solo, fitted stronger valve springs to the engine, plus a few other small modifications, then put new type, big bore, Amal carbs on it and straight through pipes. I can't remember if Geoff fitted his own Norton Wasp sidecar to this bike or if a second hand MX sidecar was bought and fitted to it, but he used this 650cc Dnieper outfit at a championship meeting in Derbyshire and won the first race on it, beating many of the top riders of the day. As it only had the standard road gearbox fitted he just drove it around for the full race in second gear.

Unfortunately, the standard road rubber drive coupling split in the next race, as it was not designed for this type of race use. What was needed was a close ratio, five speed MX gearbox, with a proper U J drive shaft joint, as we had seen fitted to the Dnieper MX outfits at the factory in Kiev. Anatol said he would try to get the competition shop in the plant to ship a pucka, five speed, close ratio race gearbox and drive shaft to us in the UK, but they did much better than this and a few months after I had sold my half of Nevals to Alan, a full 750cc Factory Works specification, complete MX outfit turned up, but by this time Geoff had split up with his sidecar championship passenger, Graham Martin, and so this full works outfit, that had arrived due to Anatol's continuous persistence in persuading the factory to send it to England, it was never put to the proper use it had been built and sent for.

The Minsk factory had air freighted a very special 125cc MX bike across to us. It was built at the State Research Institute in Moscow and was for John to test and use in MX meetings. This bike was very advanced for its time, with 12 inch front and rear suspension movement and fitted with a 32 hp 6 speed engine. The bike arrived on a Friday afternoon and on the Sunday John rode it at a Scunthorpe, open to Centre MX meeting, and he won all the three main races on it. On the next weekend at the Belchford track, near Scramblesby, he got a third and second place, but he fell off in his last race, then, two weeks later at Pickering, he got two seconds on this bike. These results shut up a lot of the Smart Alec's who looked down their noses at anything Russian. They believed only the Japanese could make winning off road bikes. It's at times like this that it's nice to prove them all wrong, after all, remember the CZ s, they stuffed it big time to the Japanese, didn't they.

I visited the Dnieper factory, this time going by train from Holland as I didn't have much faith left in Russian airlines. Me, Val, John and Derek, who worked for Nevals, went on this trip. The journey took two full days and nights, and was a great experience, and for me, preferable to flying. It was a very good visit and all of us enjoyed it. John, Val and Derek were certainly impressed by the size of the factory. On the return journey the Russian guard who checks the tickets on the train came into our compartment in tears with the news that John Lennon had just been shot in the States. It was a shock to us, but Derek's reaction didn't go down too well with the guard, who was obviously a fan and very upset.

'Well I didn't like him' said Derek. The guard

snapped something very unpleasant in Russian to him and stormed out of the compartment.

I got a very bad chest infection on my return which caused me to lay up for over three weeks. I had also recently been diagnosed as diabetic and this, on top of my heart problem caused my doctor to suggest I retire from business, because he couldn't see things getting much better for me, health wise. When Alan called in to see how I was I explained the situation to him and asked if he wanted to buy my 50% share of Nevals, the properties and stock etc. we agreed a price for the lot. Next morning he fetched me a cheque. As a business partner Alan was good to get on with and I always considered him to be a genuine friend

I was suddenly redundant after 8 years of hard work building it all up and now only a cheque in my hand to show for it. Alan transferred everything from Lincolnshire back to Hull and he acquired new premises on Holderness Road. I also signed an agreement with Alan not to deal in Russian bikes for 10 years. Anatol returned to his factory in Kiev, and before he left, me and Alan bought him a large American Ford Fairlane estate car, to take back to Kiev with him, which he filled with all sorts of expensive goods that he could sell in his home town of Kiev, at a profit. Suddenly he had become an overnight capitalist. We did hear that his boss at the factory was a bit hacked off when Anatol drove into the plant in his new car but he was promoted to number four in the factory on his return.

Within a few months I was making a steady recovery back to reasonable health. I sold the bungalow and bought a farm house and 6 acres of land just outside New Holland, called Woodbine Farm where we had some very weird experiences. We moved into the farmhouse and on the first day there, putting some furniture in place in the sitting room, there was a very strong, over powering smell of roses coming from one corner. I asked Val if she had overdone the perfume that day. She said,

'No but there did seem to be a very heavy scent of roses in here as I came in.' As I left the front room what can only be described as a dark shadow flitted across the hallway and suddenly the smell of roses had gone.

'Val' I said 'What did you make of that, I think we have a presence in this house.'

'What do you mean ?' she asked.

'Well, its something I can't explain but I think we've got a pet ghost here.' As it was to prove in the future this was correct, there was an unexplained presence in the house but it didn't feel malicious or threatening. Making alterations to the house we knocked one wall out to extend the living room into the attached barn making the living room 40ft x 20ft. When it was finished we went to Grimsby to buy a new carpet for this room and I remember jokingly saying to Val to make sure it wasn't patterned with roses.

A few days later the carpet fitter arrived and fitted the new carpet while we went out for lunch and on our return we both stood looking in total disbelief, as the entire floor was covered in a rose patterned carpet.

'Can you remember seeing any rose patterns when we bought that carpet?'

'No, I certainly didn't see any roses on the carpet when we were in the shop.' There are certain things as you go through life that seem to have no logical explanation and this was one of them. A few more odd occurrences happened with Rose, as we christened our ghost. The most bizarre was when Val went into the bathroom and both bath taps suddenly turned full on. She stood in shocked silence for 2 or 3 minutes watching the water gushing out, then finally shouted for me and as I ran up the stairs the taps just as suddenly turned off. Rose would also move things around. A large apple pie disappeared from the pantry when we had visitors and as soon as they had gone it returned to where it was originally, and no it wasn't me hiding it. On one occasion, Debbie who had asthma was unwell and I was woken by the now familiar rose smell which crossed from my side of the bed over to Val's side of the bed and back again as if to attract attention. We followed the smell which directed us to Debbie's bedroom where she was ill with a bad asthma attack. Rose was accepted as part and parcel of the house by all the family but I must admit I was relieved when we eventually moved to the shipyard house that she stayed put at Woodbine Farm. The deeds for the farm went back as far as 1646 when it was sold to a Mr William Jessop for 14 pounds cash. It listed his occupation on the deeds as a Gentleman of the first order.

Anyway back to bikes. John had bought an old Vauxhall Chevette car for bombing around our large field in, but two weeks of this and the rotten chassis fell to bits. He scrapped the bodywork but kept the engine and gearbox as it was good mechanically. I was sitting on the rear wall watching our dogs chasing each other round the field when the Chevette motor, laying on its side in the grass caught my eye and I wandered over and studied it. I brought my Ferguson diesel tractor round to lift it and carry it to my workshop where I sat the engine and gearbox upright on two bricks at the front and two at the back. I asked John 'What do you see that as?' He looked at me in an odd way and said.

'A Vauxhall engine.'

'No' I said 'look at this and I placed one of the car wheels and tyres in front of the engine and one at the back,

'Now what do you see?' Grinning he replied

'A bike, it will make a bike.' Looking at the Fergie tractor then gave me another, major idea. There is no chassis or frame on a tractor, everything just bolts onto the engine and gearbox.

Within two weeks the engine was sat in my workshop with a pair of leading link forks I had made up, bolted to the front of it, and a rear bevel box bolted on to the back of the gearbox to carry the swinging

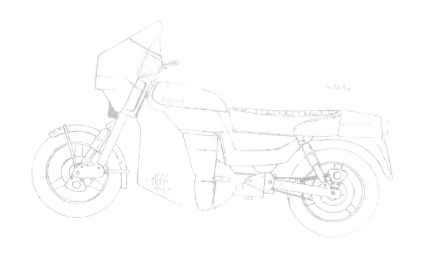

Regent, single sided suspension model
I developed with shaft drive

MOTORCYCLES
(U.K.) LIMITED

NEW HOLLAND
SOUTH HUMBERSIDE
ENGLAND
TEL. 0469 30389

Leaflet for the Regent outfit we took to the NEC Show

Don't waste your money on buying a toy When now you can buy the real McCoy REGENT

REGENT takes a fresh look at production motorcycles and sidecar outfits. Our machines are designed and built to incorporate all the ideal features a purpose built road outfit should have. At long last, a machine ideally suited to the strenuous task of sidecar work.

Both machines are fitted with the world famous GM Vauxhall Chevette type engine and gearbox, which have been in production for almost twenty years and have a time proved record for reliability, economy and low service costs. No waiting for spares either as all parts are instantly available. The motor is so good, all REGENT outfits come with a three year or 50,000 mile guarantee on the engine unit. Will any other motorcycle manufacturer offer you this?

The three-part frame and forks are constructed from heavy gauge steel box section for maximum strength and the extra wide, heavy duty tyres and wheels provide a new dimension in handling and safety as well as giving the bonus of high mileage.

The engine and gearbox form the main structure, so if you are ever unfortunate enough to damage the frame components, you just replace the actual damaged part and not the full frame. The engine is very simple to service — you don't need to drag a computer around to keep it in tune! If you are sick and tired of paying 'through the nose' for spares as well as waiting for months for them to arrive, you will find it a pleasant change for the better with a REGENT.

The reason we chose a car engine to power our bike was to bring you, the customer, what car owners have had for years, i.e. instant service and reliability, and because the engine has such high torque at low revs, only two gears are needed but if required, reverse gear can be added at no extra cost.

VERLINA
1250
T.S.R.

Forget the rest and buy the best – REGENT

SPECIFICATIONS

REGENT VERLINA 1250 T.E.		REGENT VERLINA 1250 T.S.R.	
Engine	: 4 Cylinder, water cooled.	*Engine*	: 4 Cylinder, water cooled.
Gearbox	: 2 Speed and Reverse.	*Gearbox*	: 2 Speed and Reverse.
Bore & Stroke	: 80.98mm x 60.96mm.	*Bore & Stroke*	: 80.98 x 60.96mm.
Capacity	: 1256cc.	*Capacity*	: 1256cc.
Compression	: 7.3 — 1.	*Compression*	: 9.2 — 1.
B.H.P.	: 54 @ 4,800 rpm.	*B.H.P.*	: 62.5 @ 5,400 rpm.
Carb	: Zenith 301Z.	*Carb*	: Stromburg C.D.
Firing Order	: 1 - 3 - 4 - 2.	*Firing Order*	: 1 - 3 - 4 - 2.
Suspension	: S & W Freon Socks.	*Suspension*	: S & W Air Shocks.
Tyres	: Crossply 145 x 12.	*Tyres*	: Radial 155 x 12.
Alternator	: 12 volt.	*Alternator*	: 12 volt.
Clutch	: Borg & Beck single plate.	*Clutch*	: Borg & Beck single plate.
Forks	: Regent leading link.	*Forks*	: Regent leading link.
Sidecar	: Marine ply, child adult & double adult.	*Sidecar*	: G.R.P. Occasional two seater sports.
Wheel Base	: 59".	*Wheel Base*	: 59".

Regent reserves the right to alter any of the above specifications at any time.

arm. A rear sub-frame was made and bolted on to the engine to carry the tank and seat and a special 2 x 1 wrap around box section chassis was made and attached to the engine and gearbox and hey presto, we had the makings of a sidecar outfit.

Two prototypes were made and taken to the NEC Show and we came back from the show with 117 confirmed orders for the 1250cc in line, water cooled four, Regent Verlina, as it was christened. BMW flew two of their top engineers over to the show to closely examine the bike, which had been created by me, just to stick two fingers up to certain people, but there was far more interest in it than I had expected. Unfortunately, health wise, I was not in a position to put it into production, so I pulled the plug on the project.

Both bikes were disassembled and stored under the shelves in my workshop. Both Harris and Rickman showed interest in building it but I chose to shut the project down, I had refused to take any deposits from customers at the show for bikes and so liquidated the limited company.

John, at this time used to borrow my Maico 440 to use for practicing on, keeping his own for racing.

His first meeting, riding with adults, was at Chesterfield. Brett Steel, Andy Holland, Paul Packham and many other top northern riders were surprised to be beaten that day by this 15 year old upstart, John Mason, on his Maico 440. I watched him all day as he battled with these top riders and remembered my scrambling debut at 14 on my Matchless 500cc in Lincoln so many years ago.

It was now 1983 and about a mile away from our farm, on the River Humber bank side, was a row of old cottages and a disused shipyard that covered about seven acres and had a slipway and a licence to break ships of up to 500 tons. I heard on the grapevine that it had come up for sale. Fancying a change from bikes I did the guy who owned the shipyard a deal with my New Holland Chapel and £10,000. After all I had done this type of thing before, when I bought the two barges at Beverley, many years earlier, and cut them up for scrap. At that time it was worth £6 a ton but now it was making £80 a ton. The five, two story cottages were built in 1895 and measured 120 feet long and 22 feet wide and the surveyor I used said he had never seen a building this old, as straight as this.

'They can't build them new as straight as this

John aged 15 at his first MX meeting

Me (centre) at Ripon TV meeting

now.' he said. We had all the roofs stripped off and a new roof fitted with new gutters and new windows. The inner walls were knocked through to make one big house. The living room finished up 48 feet by 22 feet, (I like big rooms). Also Mum had now moved in with us as she was getting too old to be on her own.

This turned out to be yet another right place, right time situation. The government had just instigated a decommissioning scheme for the UK fishing industry and were paying owners to scrap their boats to reduce the numbers of the UK fleet, so owners now needed somewhere to dump their boats in order to get the compensation paid to them from the government.

Around this time I had the idea to write a series of books about a Tramp his Dog and his Ferret. The books were to be called RATH, but I never did get around to completing them. Now in my retirement I have more time, so after 28 years they are finally finished and go on the world markets in SEPT 2012. The Books titles are RATH, the author is NEV MASON. It makes a very different and interesting read, following a mid 1950's Tramp's daily life and exploits travelling around England and his climb from Tramp to Tycoon. There are even a few motorcycles popping up.

THE RATH SERIES OF BOOKS

FOLLOWING THE DAILY LIFE OF A MID 1950'S TRAMP ON THE
ROAD, AND HIS EVENTUAL CLIMB FROM TRAMP TO TYCOON

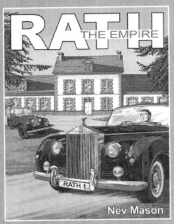

THESE BOOKS MAKE A VERY DIFFERENT READ

Series of Rath books I wrote in 2011

THE 'JOSH' SERIES OF BOOKS

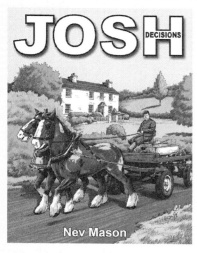

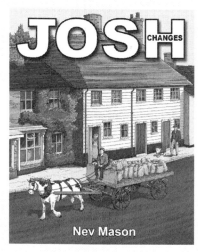

'JOSH' IS A SERIES OF 4 BOOKS FOLLOWING THE LIFE OF 15 YEAR OLD JOSH AND HIS FAMILY IN THE DIFFICULT CHANGING TIMES AFTER WORLD WAR II LIVING IN LUND IN THE YORKSHIRE COUNTRYSIDE

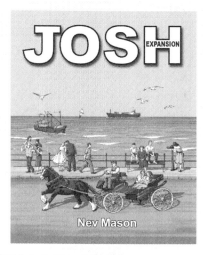

COUNTRY STORIES WITH A DIFFERENCE

Anecdote

On our very first visit to Russia we asked one of our Russian associates if Alan and I could go and look around a Russian motorcycle shop.

'Why?' Kolosov asked us.

'Because we want to see what a motorcycle shop looks and operates like here.' A quick phone call and a black Chaika limo pulled up. It was minus 22 degrees outside the large warehouse when we arrived and a long queue went around the building.

'Ah,' said Kolosov, 'there has been a new shipment of Riga mopeds just arrived.' Inside the building the queue stopped at a counter where the mopeds were paid for and the lucky buyer was given a ticket which he, in turn, gave to the salesman who was equipped with a large crow bar. He smashed open the wooden crate containing the moped and put it on its stand. The buyer then signed a paper saying that he had checked everything over and the salesman moved onto the next buyer in the queue. **Why did all these customers want to buy mopeds in this type of weather, so they could sell them and make a profit.**

Chapter 12

By 1984 the shipyard cottage conversion was finished, it had taken about a year to complete and Me, Val and Debbie along with our 7 dogs moved into our new home. John had just got married at age 20. His wife Ellen was 17 and they were given the other end of the cottages to make their home in. As I write this they have been married for 27 years and still going strong. I sold Woodbine Farm to a family from Leeds who turned it into a home for delinquent kids. (I bet Rose has her work cut out now). Within a few months of beginning to operate the shipyard we had 5 large decommissioned trawlers scattered around the waters edge of the yard. As the ship owners were getting paid the full value of their boats by the government they gave me the trawlers, as they could only be disposed of at a licensed ship breakers yard, and only two ship yards on the River Humber had these special licences. Luckily my yard was one of them.

Some heavy equipment was now needed so I bought a large Smiths 40 ton crane and a Priestman 15 ton hydraulic digger, plus a D6 Caterpillar bulldozer. I now had the job of learning how to operate them all, and I soon found that the Cat D6 would move just about anything. So, I went from motorcycle importer and designer to shipyard proprietor all in one easy lesson. I employed two casual cutters at any one time, to cut up the steel ships with oxy propane guns, and believe it or not, my daughter Debbie was the fastest cutter in the yard.

While I had the shipyard I started another revolution, this time in the eel catching industry. The shipyard and new house were on the banks of the River Humber, a really great setting with the river passing only about 100 ft from the house. When I bought the bungalow and chapel, it was from a professional eel catcher, a guy called Mick Dove who had fished for eels in the Humber and the local ponds for the last 12 years. He ran a string of Fyke nets about a mile from the yard and they stretched along the Humber for about a quarter of a mile, with a total of 126 nets and leaders. I had a Yamaha 250 Trail bike which I used to ride along the footpath on the river bank, and out one afternoon, I sat on the bike for about two hours watching Mick start at one end of the line of nets and work all the way to the other end, emptying the catch from each net. It all looked hard work and when he

Me and John talking on the Smiths crane

Some of the ships we broke up at the yard

finally had his catch on the bank top I couldn't believe that out of 126 nets he had only caught 38 eels. As well as this he now had to go back along the line of nets and repair about forty of them that were damaged. I watched him start repairing the nets for a while and then rode back along the bank and home.

As I had my tea, Val and I sat on our big wooden balcony which overlooked the fast flowing River Humber. I wasn't taking in the scenery as Val was, I was thinking about eels.

What if half inch steel mesh, about three foot high and thirty feet long was placed across the current, instead of down the current as everybody else seemed to lay their leaders out. Mick had already told me that eels, in rivers with strong currents, always travel with the current and if they meet an obstacle they would turn and follow it towards the middle of the river.

The next day I went across to Hull and bought three lengths of galvanised half inch steel mesh, 3ft by 30 ft. Putting my shipyard wellies on I took one length of mesh and 4 wooden posts to the riverside. The first post was put at the top waterline then one post hammered in every ten feet and the mesh nailed on with 1 inch galvanised staples. No way was the tide going to move this. The second mesh panel was put in line across the current behind the first and secured with four more wooden posts. Then I made two mesh boxes using the same steel mesh, 2ft high x 2ft wide x 3ft long. Val sewed onto one end of each box, a normal string mesh cone, 2 ft long tapering down to 2 inches on the inner end, to funnel the eels into the mesh box so they couldn't find their way out again. A steel mesh opening hatch was fitted to the opposite end to be used, hopefully, to remove the catch through. The two boxes were fitted, one to each of the 30ft steel leaders that pointed towards the centre of the river. They looked impressive all set up but would they work.

The next morning I was up at 6 o'clock, half an hour after the tide turned and both nets were uncovered. When I went out to check them, the top net had 43 eels and 4 flatfish in it and the second, had 57 eels and 11 flatfish, so my two nets had caught 100 eels compared to Mick's 38 eels from his 126 Fyke nets. Over the next 2 months I extended the mesh fence out 270 feet into the river. The biggest catch one late August morning was 2 cwt of eels in one tide plus over one cwt of flatfish. All this from only nine mesh holding boxes.

A guy I knew from Hull used to come to collect the catch every day, and after a months trial I asked the guy to remove the steel mesh line, and gave him the lot, FOC. He dismantled it and took it all across to Hull and reassembled it in the River Humber near the Fish Docks, where it stayed for many years.

The only reason I did all this was simply to test my theory and prove to myself that a better and different method of eel fishing, than the conventional one used by everybody else, could be devised. Word soon got around about my low maintenance, low cost, steel mesh system and the yard had visitors every now and then from other curious eel fisherman who came to check out the new system they had heard about but they had to be redirected across to Hull to view the working model. I am told this in line steel fence method is now used in many parts of the country to catch eels and fish.

At the same time as my eel experiment, John was running his own business building and selling the Regent sidecars which had been developed originally for the Regent Verlina outfits. He also sold and fitted the Regent leading link fork conversions and 12 inch wheel kits that had been developed for the Regent

Verlina outfits as well. He made and fitted these special Regent, side by side, sidecars and fork and wheel kits to his customers own Guzzies, Harley Davidsons and Gold Wings etc. so at least part of the Regent got onto the market. He ran this service for about two years and sold about 110 sidecars and 75 fork and wheel kits and in this time and he also made and sold 6 brand new, complete, Regent Honda CX 650cc sidecar outfits. These were tested by Motor Cycle News and Motor Cycling magazine who both said they drove and handled brilliantly.

John had a customer from Scotland who wanted a new Regent sidecar and a Regent fork and wheel conversion fitted on his Guzzi and he stayed at our house until it was finished two days later. He worked at Marine Harvest one of the major producers of farmed salmon on Scotland. He asked, with me having a shipyard, if we made boats but I said no, at the moment we only cut up decommissioned ships for scrap. I asked him why he wanted to know and he said that the fish farms in Scotland had problems with their service boats, as they were made of fibreglass, and every time there was a storm in the lochs they were losing boats at an alarming rate and had been for years. They were

Four of the many Regent sidecars and small wheel conversions we made

Regent Ultimate sidecar fitted to a Harley Davidson

getting smashed up on the rocks, and what they really needed were steel boats to stand up to this heavy work. The major problem was the boats had to be fast and it would appear that no one in the UK had ever thought about making a fast but strong 20 foot steel work boat.

After the customer had returned to Scotland with his new outfit me and John sat one evening talking about making small fast steel boats.

'What do we know about designing boats?' John asked. 'Nothing.' I replied.

'That's why we can do it, to start with, we don't have any preconceived ideas about how it should be made or what it should look like, so we can start with a clean slate.' We agreed to make a prototype boat and we started to lay out the guide lines, the requirements were to be;

1. Maximum length at water level, 17 foot.
2. Maximum length top line, 20 foot.
3. Flat bottom for working off loch sides.
4. Carrying capacity minimum half ton.
5. Buoyancy tanks, welded in, fore and aft.
6. Hull bottom in 5mm plate.
7. Sides and tanks in 3mm plate.
8. Minimum top speed with 40hp outboard, 25 knots

9. Stand up forward cuddy.
10. 4 inch x 4 inch rubber bumper mounted on front for pushing the fish cages.

We both spent time over the next week sketching our ideas and comparing them. We eventually arrived at a basic shape, incorporating ideas from us both and John spent the next few days cutting out plywood templates which were then bolted together so at least we could see what it would look like. The shape looked quite pleasing so we ordered enough of the required size steel to make one hull. John, who doesn't believe in doing things by half disappeared to the local Machine Mart and came back with a brand new £1500 Mig welder.

The first attempt at cutting the steel proved that oxy propane cutting was not the answer as the heat from this made the plates buckle and twist. So, back to Machine Mart and another £1200 was spent on a metal plate cropper which literally does what it says, bites its way along the metal a quarter of an inch at a time in continuous bites. With this time proved, cold mechanical system, there is no distortion or twisting of the plate being cut and it could also cut very tight radiuses. Unfortunately its down side was that you needed to wear ear muffs as it was very noisy.

John had designed the bottom and sides so they were self hung, so when they were tacked into place they assumed the shape they would on the boat. Most steel boats are normally made upside down on a steel jig but our system didn't require any jig at all and as it was built the right way up it was self shaping. The bottom, instead of being completely flat was lifted at the front by two bricks. One placed either side at the front. (bricks are very handy things), and then placing one brick each side at the back it now had the required bottom shape we were looking for. Over the next week the whole boat was short tacked together. John devised a building system so that when the hull was fully welded it wasn't distorted. This was achieved by first, tack welding the panels on the left hand side, then the right hand side panels were tack welded. This swapping equally from side to side pulled the hull back straight each time. Using this method the whole hull was welded inside and out. We then designed and fitted new reversed top chines on the hull which locked the whole hull into position.

It now looked like a boat, so it was taken to the boat yard and put into the water to see how it performed. Part of the shipyard was a 3 acre pond and this was where all the initial testing was done. It was lowered into the water with my Priestman excavator which had a long reach arm fitted. It floated for the first time and as we climbed into it to fit the 40hp Mariner outboard onto it, we were surprised how stable the hull was.

With the motor fitted we fired it up and a slow trip across the pond was made. It all seemed OK. I got out and asked John to go a bit faster while I watched from the bank side to see how it was riding in the water. Under half power two things were immediately apparent. First it pushed its bow up in the air the faster it went and second it slid sideways across the water when put into a fast turn. John also reported that the 2 inch by a quarter, steel ribs fitted across the floor were causing the floor to move up and down as the hull bottom hit the swell caused by going round the pond.

We took the boat back to the workshop and all the internal floor ribs were taken out and the boat turned upside down. A length of 2" x 2" T section was then welded onto the full length of the hull down the centre line, upside down with the T part facing downwards. Two more T sections were welded two and a half feet to either side of the centre T section. This should stop the hull bottom moving and give some grip on the water when turning fast I thought, also, without the internal ribs the floor inside was now flat with nothing to trip up over.

What a difference when it was back in the water. Now it cornered like a speed boat because not only were the upside down T sections stopping the boat sliding across the water sideways but they had also stopped completely the floor movement. One addition had solved two problems. An added bonus with the reversed T section welded on to the bottom of the hull, was that it now tracked and steered very positively when going straight ahead, just like it was running on rails.

Near to us was a water ski centre and after putting the boat back into the workshop me and John went to look at the speed boats being used on the water ski ponds. The first thing we saw was that the fibreglass hulls ran more level the faster they went. In the ski centre shop there was a boat with a four inch wide metal flap fitted right across the back, level with the bottom of the hull. Once we were back in our workshop we made a four inch by a quarter, adjustable flap. It was fitted across the full width of the stern with four hinges and set at a one inch angle downwards, secured with two adjustable rods. We went to try it on our pond and at three quarter throttle the front only ran about nine inches out of the water instead of the previous two foot. We adjusted the angle further to two inches and this time the front of the boat when at speed started to push down into the water like a submarine, soaking John with the resulting bow wave.

Trim Tabs, as we later learned they were called, are fitted to most fast fibreglass speed boats but it seems nobody had thought to use them on small steel work boats before. We now set the angle to one and a half inches down and this setting was spot on, and the hull ran level at speed and now did everything that was required of it.

Back again at the workshop the flat 4 inch steel plate was welded to the hull at an angle of one and a half inches and on re-testing we had a very fast steel hull that did everything it should do. It was fast with fantastic cornering abilities, ran level at speed and was very stable and strong. The next week we built a brand new hull incorporating all the improvements and modifications that had been made on boat number one, plus the addition of welded in buoyancy tanks, fore and aft. It was shot blasted and painted red, then we ran tests on it for about a month in the River Humber, including filling it with water to try to sink it, but it just sat there, very low in the water but still floating.

Matthew from the Ski Club came and tested it and he could not believe a steel hull could do all this. He rated the handling and manoeuvrability as good as any of fibreglass boats used at the Ski centre.

Two weeks later John rang the Guzzi man in Scotland and asked him if he could arrange an appointment for John to meet the buyer at Marine Harvest's depot near Oban, so he could show him our new steel boat design which we believed should be just what they are looking for. He managed to get John the appointment, so we hired a Ford Cargo, 7 ton truck, to take the Regent 20 as we had christened the boat, to Scotland for a demo at the Salmon Farm.

They were very impressed with all its capabilities and John stayed with them for two days while they put it through its paces. A full thumbs up was given by the management. John was asked the price and he told them £1495 with a forward cuddy fitted or £1295 without a cuddy. They wanted him to leave the boat with them for a full week of testing so he rang to check with me and I said it was OK to leave it.

John got back late on the Friday night and on the following Tuesday morning someone rang from Marine Harvest to say that on the Sunday night there had been a violent storm and 11 of their fleet of 15 fibre glass boats had broken from their moorings and had been dashed against the rocks at the loch end and were smashed to bits. He also added, as an after thought.

'The Regent 20 you left with us to test also finished up on the rocks but apart from a few dents and scratches it's OK, we pulled it off the rocks and it's here now working on the cages. If we order 20 now how soon can you deliver them to us?' We said we would ring back and me and John set about working out a realistic delivery date for them. John said he thought he could have one full hull a day finished but to allow a second day for shot blasting and painting. I told John to ring them back and tell them we could deliver all the 20 in a maximum of 6 weeks. This was agreed and they said they would organise a cheque for half the total amount as a deposit with the balance to be paid on the completed delivery.

REGENT STEEL WORK BOATS

TOUGH STEEL WORKBOATS DEVELOPED ESPECIALLY FOR FISH FARMING AT AN AFFORDABLE PRICE

20ft Open Hull

Left:
23ft Flat
Bottomed
Planeing
Hull

Right:
23ft Shallow
Vee Semi
Displace-
ment
Hull

23ft Hulls, one with Forward Cuddy

SIZE	HULL PRICE	SHOT BLASTING & PRIMING	BOUYANCY TANKS FORE & AFT	BOUYANCY TANKS SIDE	CUDDY	EXTRA BEAM
16' x 6' x 2½'	£895	£100	£150	—	£295	—
18' x 7' x 3'	£1195	£125	£160	—	£395	—
20' x 7' or 8' x 3'	£1295	£135	£175	—	£420	£100
23' x 7' or 8' x 3'	£1495	£150	£200	£200	£495	£100
23' x 8' x 4'	£1895	£165	£200	£200	£495	—
(SHALLOW VEE HULL)						

Regent high speed steel work boat leaflet

Regent 20 - the high speed steel work boat we developed

That's how it all started, my top cutter in the shipyard, Debbie my daughter now became John's top Mig welder on the steel boat production. The first 10 hulls were delivered in less than three weeks and when other Salmon Farms saw them they all wanted them and orders started pouring in. We even supplied 15 Regent 20's to the big docklands project at Canary Wharf, in London to be used as fast work boats.

Many so called experts in the boat building industry said steel boats could not be made to perform the way the Regent 20 does, but we proved them all wrong. Slowly John's boat business took over from the sidecar business. His sidecar mould was reaching the end of its production life and it would be very expensive and time consuming to have a new mould made so the decision was made to concentrate on the boat building. He also developed a slightly bigger version of the Regent 20 boat to add to his range, the Regent 25. John made them and I sold them. This system worked well for us both and did not conflict with my boat yard work.

Now many years later, copies of the Regent 20, the boat that me and John designed in less than two weeks, are still being made worldwide in Russia, India and China. They are the main producers of this fast steel, 20 foot boat. We know this because we gave the motorcycle factories we were working with the drawings, FOC for the Regent 20 design and they then farmed the construction out to other factories in their own countries on a royalty basis.

KEEP CLIMBING THE LADDER NEV, IF YOU STOP YOU WILL GO BACK DOWN AGAIN.
QUOTE FROM HENRY HALL CUSHWORTH'S DONCASTER.

Nev Mason
saying
1986
One of the enjoyments in life is proving that many of the so called experts were wrong

Chapter 13

It was now July1988 and I had really enjoyed the past three and a half years, and so had John. It had been a refreshing change working with boats, and helping John part time with his Regent motor cycle business. My health was now quite good, helped by the exercise, driving, and climbing in and out of the heavy equipment at the shipyard.

There was not much time left now to run on my 10 year agreement with Alan. The Russians had been in contact with me every year since my departure from Nevals to enquire about restarting our cooperation, and me selling the Russian bikes again for them, so I put an advert in the local paper for my house and land to see if there was any interest in it. The next day I got a phone call from a Mr Billy Forester at Omega Windows of Lincoln who wanted to come and look at the property and he arrived the next day with his brother Steve Forester. They spent about two hours going around the house and land.

'Yes we like it' Billy said, 'would you take a bid on it?'

'Try me.' I answered.

'We will offer you £120,000 for it.' Part of me wanted to say yes OK but my business side instantly stopped that decision.

'No' I found myself saying 'It's got to be £125,000 or leave it.'

'OK' he said 'we will buy it at that give me your solicitors address.' which I did and they were gone. A day later a phone call from Billy Forester asked if I would sell the Smiths crane in the yard.

'Yes' I said.

'How much for it?' he asked.

'£5000' I replied. This was, even for me, all moving a bit fast.

The next week a letter from my solicitors arrived with all the relevant paperwork which Val and I completed and returned, and a week after that we were informed that the deposit had been received and the Foresters wanted to complete within one month, so it seems they were very serious about buying.

There were two ships left in the yard still to cut up so I rang a mate of mine in Hull and offered him and his brother 30 percent of all that they cut up. This was agreed and they arrived the next day and started work on the remaining ships, saving me from having to cut them up myself, I just operated the big Smiths crane for them. Just down the road from us was Gissing's, a car scrap yard and house that was for sale, so I went down to have a look at it. The house had 3 bedrooms and 4 acres of land which was full of scrap cars and other junk. I bought it from Gissing for £90,000 complete with all the stock, just as it all stood, and set the completion date for one months time. But people never fail to amaze me, five days after we shook hands on the deal John passed Gissing coming out of the yard with his transit van down on its knees, loaded with valuable gear he was moving out, before the sale went through. I waited until I saw his empty van return and then gave him a ring. His wife answered the phone and went to get him.

'Mr Gissing, its Nev from the shipyard, do you really want to sell your place?' I asked him. There was a stunned silence from his end which was then followed by.

'What do you mean?' I was short and sharp with him.

'Please put all that gear you took out of the yard in your transit back or the deal is off.'

'How do you know, who told you?' he said

thereby incriminating himself.

'I can see your yard entrance from here, I've been watching you moving it.' He had it all back within the day.

Billy came down one day, prior to the completion date. He had brought a lot of gear in an Omega Window's work van and asked if he could leave it in an empty downstairs room in the house. It was no problem to me so he unloaded it then said he would see me tomorrow and left. At eleven o'clock the next day I rang my solicitors to see if the remainder of the money had been transferred across to him.

'It came in five minutes ago.' he replied, 'You've been paid ok.'

'Good, can you pay for Gissing's house out of this money now please?'

'No problem Nev I will see to it right away for you.' That night me, Val, Deb and our seven dogs spent the night in a 10 foot long caravan borrowed from my friend Dave Jackson. John and his wife Ellen went to stay with relatives. After a rather cramped night in the caravan, even the dogs looked pi....d off, so we all piled into the van and set off for a Little Chef. We settled the dogs down in the back of the van with food and water and me, Val and Deb went inside and had the all day breakfast. I asked Val what she had thought of living in a small caravan but I can't put in print what her reply was.

Back at the yard where the caravan still was, the Foresters had arrived with a van load of household goods, and seeing us they asked where we had stayed that night, so I pointed to the caravan.

'I thought you had bought the house at the scrap yard.' Steve said.

'I have' I replied 'but according to my solicitor, up to last night the money hadn't gone through. I'm going to ring again later to check.'

My mate from Hull was now about three quarters of the way through the ship cutting job and there was just one more boat to cut up. It was a tug which I told the Foresters would take them about two weeks to finish and they were OK with this. I spent about three hours lifting large sections cut from the ships onto the bank for the cutters to reduce to 3 foot by 2 foot pieces. A very fed up Val and Deb were sat in the caravan looking after our seven restless dogs, so I went down to Gissing's at about 2 o'clock to ask if he had any news of the money going through, but he said that he had telephoned his solicitor only ten minutes previously and it was still not there. He had been told to ring again at 4 o'clock.

I had been back at the yard for about an hour, working the Smiths crane, loading some second hand marine engines I had sold and were being collected to go for reconditioning. As soon as I had finished I went back to see Gissing again. He rang his man who confirmed that the money had come through at 2.30. So now the property was legally mine and had been since half past two. There was no way I was sleeping in that caravan for another night so I asked Gissing, politely, to please move out and at 5 o'clock me, Val, Deb and the dogs were at the yard, moving our stuff into the house at one side as the Gissing's were moving their stuff out at the other side.

It took us about an hour, with John, Ellen and Debbie's help to get the basics in and the kettle on for a drink. Gissing came back for his third load and was then gone for good. A cup of tea was welcome after the hectic last few hours. I don't think I have ever seen Val look so pleased or relieved to be in a house again and the dogs seemed to like the new place too. Over the next few days I finished clearing all our personal belongings from the old house and Val arranged everything in the new house. It felt like we had a home again.

I had put a large notice on the gate saying the scrap yard was to be closed for a month, but I had no intention of operating it as a scrap yard and the next three months would be spent clearing all the scrap cars and junk out of the yard.

I kept the Cat D 6 Bulldozer from the shipyard which I now used to take the top six inches off the four acre yard in order to get rid of all the accumulated half buried rubbish and remove the soil and debris, which was now used to form a bank round the land. Three months after the big clean up it didn't look like there had ever been a scrap yard on the site.

I didn't start smoking until I was 19 but by now I was a heavy smoker and as I got older it was starting to be a problem. About 6 months after moving to Gissing's I was taken into Scunthorpe hospital with a blood clot in my thigh, which had become twice its normal size. I had emergency surgery to remove the clot and afterwards was told to either stop smoking or I had about two months left to live. The doctor said.

'But its your life Mr Mason and frankly I

couldn't care less whether you live or die, if you don't care, then why should I?' I had tried, unsuccessfully, for many years to stop smoking, now I stopped instantly and have never smoked since, or ever wanted to.

John applied for and got planning permission to have a new bungalow built on a two acre section of the yard, after we split the land in two down the middle, and four months later a large new bungalow sat on the right hand side of the site. John and Ellen moved into the bungalow at Christmas 1989. We put the original house and the two acres it stood on up for sale for £95,000 and within two months had accepted an offer of £90,000 for it. Me and Val along with Debbie moved into the bungalow with John and Ellen, which had been built in a large U shape around a court yard.

John had extended an already large steel shed which was on the bungalows land where he now manufactured his steel boats while the original part of the shed was used for the new Regent bike business. John wanted to develop this side of the building to start the Regent Motocross Shop so we went to see Bill Brown, an old friend who was the importer of Maico motocross bikes and the manufacturer of Wulfsport motocross clothing. We bought two new Maico 500cc bikes for stock for the new MX shop and took on a Wulfsport distributor agreement to sell and develop the clothing sales. We also bought a 1987 Honda CR250, a 1988 Kawasaki KX 125 and a 1986 Kawasaki KX 250 and these plus the two Maico 500's completed the stock we started the business with.

We opened for the first time on a Saturday and even I was surprised by the amount of customers that turned up to buy the Wulfsport MX clothing. All the second hand bikes were sold and one of the new Maico's. Because we were Wulfsport wholesale/distributors we made double the profit we would have done just as a dealer and this was undeniably a good business to be in, and to expand, by distributing to other shops in our area.

There was obviously a shortage of second hand motocross bikes in the area judging by the amount of people coming into the shop looking to buy one, and it was starting to look just like the old days in bikes, and it was off to Doug Hacking's to buy used MX bikes for stock and then on to Bill Browns again for some more, by the following week we had fourteen used bikes in the showroom to sell.

It makes you wonder just what idiots would think of opening a moto cross shop in the middle of nowhere, miles from any town, well we DID and it worked very well for us. If you have what the customers want and you look after them they will find you no matter where your business is located. Bill Brown also proved my theory right, as his top selling Cumbrian motorcycle shop was located in the middle of an old disused quarry, but he still out sold all the other dealers in his area.

The Regent moto cross shop took off like a rocket and we were now out selling most of the other UK Wulfsport dealers with the full range of moto cross clothing. Our biggest problem was finding and buying the large amounts of second hand bikes that we needed. We solved this problem by bulk buying from mainly southern dealers who had loads of used bikes in stock which they couldn't shift. We bought a brand new Iveco, twin wheeled, van which would carry up to 15 bikes, and even pull a trailer if required. Main dealers for Suzuki, Honda, Yamaha and Kawasaki were our best suppliers, as they had the biggest stocks of bikes they had taken in part exchange against new bikes, and they all had big bills to pay to their importers every

Top: Shows amount of stock we kept at Regent MX shop
Bottom: Aerial view of Regent MX and the new bungalow

1991 Regent MX race team

month. Our bulk buying was the answer to many of their problems and it gave them large amounts of money and, more importantly to them, instant cash flow. Two deals stick in my mind. Terry Rudd Honda Centre in South Lincolnshire had 18 late bikes he wanted to sell, so me and John went to see them. They were all nice, clean, well maintained bikes and I was just about to bid him £23,500 for the lot when he said that the Honda importer wanted a cheque from him on Monday for £18,500 he owed them. Well, I looked at John to see if he had picked up what I had, and I saw that he had, so the bid just had to be £18,000 didn't it?

'I can't take that I've got £27,200 in them.'

'OK, my last bid £18,500.' I bought them all for this amount saving £5000 on what I was originally going to bid him. He really should not have given me that information. The second I clearly remember, was at John Banks Honda Centre in Cambridge. His sons Mark and Justin were running the shop and they had 19 second hand bikes to trade out, again all good tidy machines. We bought them all for £19,500 and as we were loading them into the van Mark picked out a CR250.

'That bike was stolen from us last week' he said

to Justin.

'I took it in part exchange yesterday.' Justin replied 'and I gave the guy a real good part exchange allowance on it against a new CR500.' We paid them the £19,500 for the bikes and left the still arguing brothers to sort it out between themselves.

Word had started to get around that Regent MX were buying large numbers of second hand MX bikes and dealers were ringing up with lists of bikes to sell. Even Honda got in on the act when a guy called Dave Dunham from Louth contacted us and said that Neal Tuxworth at the Honda UK's workshops in Louth had a fair amount of ex championship, sponsored riders bikes to sell. John went to see them and came back with a couple of the ex works Honda CR 250's that Dave Dunham had mentioned, and a week later Neal rang John to say he had another 9 ex works Honda's at Louth to sell. We bought these bikes and over that year we must have bought about 120 ex works Honda CR125's, 250's and 500's from Honda UK. They were locating and collecting bikes from all over the country, that were still in the possession of some of their sponsored riders, then sold them on to us.

These bikes were very popular with our Regent

John and Wayne's new 250 MX CR Hondas

Caught napping in Russia's 40 degree heat

MX customers because, being ex works bikes, they had been very well looked after and maintained mechanically. We ourselves sponsored our own Regent MX team with these ex Honda UK bikes and cleaned up just about every meeting within 75 miles of our shop. Riders sponsored by Regent on these Hondas included; Shaun Sykes, Kenny Wyatt, John Mason, Tristan Buckley and Wayne Leaning and they all had brilliant results on them. Wayne Leaning, was a lad who lived near the Regent shop. He started working full time for us and ended up staying with us for about 14 years.

Every time Honda had bikes to sell they would ring us. They had some ex Display Team Honda XR 250's to sell, 12 of them, and 10 ex Road Race, Training School, Honda 400's so we took a trip to London where they were stored and bought them all. It took two trips to bring them back to the shop. The XR 250's were advertised in the local paper and the amount of interest in them was unbelievable.

At 9 o'clock on the Saturday morning following the Friday night advert, Wayne went to open the outer gate and there were 9 vehicles parked outside all with customers waiting, wanting to buy XR 250 Hondas. 10

were sold within 15 minutes of opening the shop. There were only two left and two lads were fighting in the yard outside over who was next in line and going to buy them. The biggest lad won the argument and bought both the last two XR 250's. We had never seen anything like this before, fighting over who was here first.

Whenever we sold a MX bike, new or second hand, we always gave the customer a free, new Regent Wulfsport MX race shirt, and on this occasion we gave the loser a free shirt as well as consolation for missing out on the Honda XR 250's. These Wulfsport Regent MX race shirts became mega popular and at one meeting at Newbald, just in one race alone, of the 26 riders on the start line 23 were wearing a Regent Wulfsport racing shirt.

Neal Tuxworth rang us and asked if we would be interested in sponsoring one of their Honda riders, Stuart Coyle, in all the British and World Championship rounds. Honda would provide us with six new CR 500's for Stuart, free of charge, plus the engine running spares for the 1991 season. Regent would provide Stuart with tyres, Wulfport race clothing, his race transport, and a mechanic. Regent would be the first ever non franchised Honda dealership to sponsor a Honda works rider in the championships but Honda did try hard to get us to become an official franchised dealer at a meeting on their 'Dealer Day' at Hawkstone Park.

The meeting went like this;

'We would like Regent MX to become our official Honda distributors for Honda MX bikes for Lincolnshire.'

'What does that entail?' I asked.

'Honda UK would expect you to paint your shop in Honda Corporate colours, we would then instruct you how to run the shop and Regent must buy a minimum of 50 new bikes a year from us'

'Can I choose the models I buy?' I asked.

'No, we tell you what models you have to buy.' their representative replied.

'Sorry but I'm not interested.' I said and got to my feet and headed for the door. A stunned table full of Honda executives watched as I reached the door saying

'Come on John.' who with Wayne was still sitting at the table. 'We are going.'

I tried to open the door, not realising it was a sliding door, it resisted, so I grabbed it and pulled harder, pulling it right off its fittings. I was now stood there holding the complete door in my hands so I gently propped it against the wall and then walked out through the resulting aperture.

'That's that, Honda won't want us to sponsor Stuart now.' said a disappointed John and Wayne. But surprise, surprise, on the following Monday morning a large bunch of flowers arrived at the shop from Honda UK with a message saying that Honda were very sorry that Mr No-Name had upset me at the Hawkstone Dealer Day meeting but would we still like to buy their second hand MX bikes and run Stuart Coyle in the Championships for them. Yes was the answer we gave them and we had good, long term dealings with Neal Tuxworth and Honda UK for many years after that.

With Stuart Coyle you always got commitment and concentration on the job he was doing for Regent MX, both on and off the track, he was a real top rider and a top person. We sponsored him again the year after the Honda deal, on full Works Maicos in the World and British championships in conjunction with Bill Brown's Wulfsport business. His riding ability had not diminished nor his commitment to racing. There are not many riders that could arrive at the start line

Stuart Coyle on Regent Honda 500

Top: Debbie and Kenny Wyatt on works Maico at York Show
Bottom: John winning the Championship race at Pickering

last, then get the hole shot and be leading by the first corner, but Stuart could do that time after time. His mind set was truly amazing, he just never gave up.

For the Czechoslovakian Grand Prix we developed and built a special 465cc engine for the Maico he rode at this meeting, using parts from Maico, Honda and Kawasaki engines. With this special engine fitted he got the fastest time of the day at this World Grand Prix meeting. Stuart always praised the Maico's handling, he could not believe just how good it was, but he was very heavy on engines and gear boxes and this is why we built this extra strong engine for him.

We finished 1992 running him in all the remaining championships on Kawasaki Works KX500 bikes supplied FOC to us at Regent MX by Kawasaki Motors UK, as the Maicos Stuart had been using continued to have gearbox and clutch problems.

We sponsored him again a few years later on Colin Hill's Husaberg 500cc four strokes. He may have been a bit older but his ultra aggressive riding style still frightened the life out of many of the other top runners in the Championships.

Nev Mason
saying
1991
*They say the best things in life are free but
experience will show you they ain't*

Anecdote

'Nev are you interested in buying some of our Russian vodka which is made in Minsk?' Sash asked me, 'It's strong stuff, about forty five percent proof the factory that makes it says.'

'How much is it a bottle?' I asked him.

'Only fifty cents a bottle and they can get quite a few thousand bottles into a 40 foot container but the minimum order,' he added, 'is for twenty 40 foot containers at a time.'

'No thanks Sash. I just fancied a few bottles for myself. **I didn't want to buy enough to share with the rest of England.**'

Chapter 14

The Regent MX shop continued to grow with customers coming from all over the county to buy bikes and clothing. One day a phone call came from a very happy sounding Russian, it was Kolosov ringing me from Moscow.

'Nev your 10 year agreement with Alan finishes tomorrow.' a quick look at the calendar confirmed he was correct. 'Can you fly across next week to see us?'

'Ring me back in an hour.' I told him 'I'll talk to John' I then rang Harold Lawson, a friend in Grimsby, who had expressed a desire to go to the Minsk factory, if I ever visited Russia again, and he said he would love to go with me and John so when Kolosov rang me back I said.

'If we fly, we're not going on any Russian planes, and while in Russia we only travel on the trains.'

'That's OK Nev, it's no problem.' I was very relieved when the tickets came to see British Airways on them.

The landing at Moscow Airport was a better experience than the last time I'd arrived there on a

Russian plane. Mr Kolovos picked us up at the airport and we spent the night at the same massive Hotel Ukraine opposite the Russian Houses of Parliament in central Moscow, as on my and Alan's trip years earlier.

Mid morning we were picked up and taken to Avtoexport's new offices where we had an interesting meeting with many of the guys from years ago, but there was no sign of the possible double agent Oleg. Mr Kolasov and Mr Safonov took us to lunch in a big posh restaurant near their offices and the five course meal took four hours to complete. Then it was back to the hotel to get five hours of rest before catching the over night train to Minsk. A car arrived to take us to the station and Kolasov accompanied us to Minsk.

When we arrived, there was a delegation waiting to greet us, and we were taken to the Planeta Hotel where more people awaited us, and everybody sat down to lunch. I counted around the table, including me, John and Harold 47 people, and at the head of the table was Constantine Ustymchuk, the new director of the Minsk factory, who was formally introduced to us. In this type of circumstance the Russians, or Byelorussians as they insist on being called, know how to have a good time and make things last. We sat down at 12 noon and got up from the table to leave at 7.30 p.m.

The next morning Harold looked ill, a case of too much vodka and John didn't look too bright either. I was OK as I had used Anatol's method of getting rid of the vodka. At one o'clock we were transported to the factory by a fleet of cars and were greeted at the factory entrance by a small crowd waving Union Jack flags as we swept through the gates. The new director welcomed us to his big new office and all the top staff were round the long gleaming conference table, including the previous director's son, Vsevold Klenikski, who was now the chief designer at the factory. He knew what we had achieved with the Minsk many years ago and wanted to work with us to continue this theme. He was to become another great personal friend. If a Russian accepts you as a friend then you have a genuine friend for life.

A full tour of the plant impressed John and Harold but I had seen it all before. We had a long meeting with Mr Klenikski Senior and his son Vsevolod (or Sev as we now called him) covering all aspects, even though Klenikski Senior was not the main director anymore he obviously still carried a great deal of influence in the factory.

They had laid on a moto cross practice day for John and introduced their top rider, Volodya Eseavich to us. The Minsk plant sponsored him with two new CR Honda 125's to race and he lent one of these to John to ride. It was a good day and even Harold enjoyed it. I managed to scrounge a CR 125 Honda for about half an hour to the consternation of everyone. Many of the on lookers wanted to know who the old fat guy blowing off many of the younger riders was. I have to confess it was ME, when I stopped Sev came across grinning widely.

'That was very, very good Nev. Now they have seen you ride like that, at your age, it will give them all a new respect for you.'

Back at the factory Ustymchuk asked us how many motocross riders we sponsored in the UK.

'10' was my answer.

'Why don't you bring them over here to Minsk for a special motocross meeting, England v Belarus. Motovelo will pay for all the accommodation and food expenses in Minsk for your team.' We agreed to think about it when we returned to the UK.

Sev showed us a new fairing he had designed for

the Minsk but explained that the management wouldn't let him put it into production as they said it was far to expensive to make. I suggested he buy the prototype from them and have it made outside the factory and sell it in the sports shops in the city. This he did, and overnight he became another converted capitalist entrepreneur, I understand he sold quite a lot of them in the Minsk area.

Bidding our farewells we boarded the overnight train back to Moscow where we had another meeting at Avtoexport to agree on prices etc. and then it was back onto the British Airways plane to the UK.

The turbulence on the flight back was horrendous, with torrential rain, and I thought it was just the Russian planes that handled like this. When we finally landed at Heathrow all the passengers cheered the pilot for his skill in landing the aircraft. I decided there and then, I would definitely be travelling by train in the future for my visits to Russia.

Back at the shop business returned to normal, we bought a load of Suzuki's and Kawasaki's from K S MX, at St Leonards on Sea, and 8 new KTM's and nine second hand KTM's from Gordon Jones, the KTM importer. All our sponsored riders were asked if they fancied going to Russia to ride in a challenge MX meeting and most said yes they would go as it would be a world first opportunity for them.

Del Stanley, from the Hull Bike Training School offered to take his large Mercedes van as it would carry most of the bikes and a new Transit van Regent had recently bought was to be used to transport the riders and gear in. There was a lot of paperwork to sort out but only a few months after our last visit, there we were, setting off to drive to Minsk.

On the map it didn't look to be very far but of course it was. All went well until our first major hiccup which occurred at the main border crossing between Poland and Russia. The guards refused entry into Belarus to the team as, according to them, the documents were not correct, but a Regent MX shirt and two copies of the glossy Dirt Bike Rider magazine given to them, brought about a change of mind. We were then waved through the barriers. After two and a half days driving we finally arrived on the outskirts of Minsk. We stopped at a phone box and rang Sev to ask him to inform Ustymchuk that we would all be arriving at the Planeta Hotel in about one hour. When we did finally get to the hotel, the right people were waiting to show the party to their rooms. They organised food and drink for us all and placed an armed guard around our vans to protect the bikes.

The following morning everybody had breakfast and then it was off to a practice session at the track which was about ten kilometres from Minsk. All our riders met most of their riders and all walked round the track to inspect it. The first set of practice laps went OK, but during the second set of practice laps I was informed by Sev that John and Pete Ralph, one of out Regent riders, had come off and hurt themselves. I was asked if I could take our Transit van over to where they were. When I got there it looked a lot worse than I expected. About 7 riders were scattered around the track. I spotted John who was laid on his right side with his left leg pointing the opposite way to what it should have been pointing. The same thing seemed to have happened to Pete Ralph's arm which was angled backwards. It seemed one of the Russian riders had come off in a dip, and because he and the bike lay over the brow of the hill, the other riders couldn't see him on their approach and had landed on top of him. He was in a bad way.

'Sev' I asked 'where are the Ambulance guys?'

There were none in attendance at the scene of the accident.

'I haven't seen any since I arrived.' he confirmed, so me and Sev, and some of the other riders had no option but to load all the injured riders into the transit van and we set of for the hospital. Our top speed was restricted to about 25 mph as the country roads were very bad and it took about 20 minutes to get there but I must admit that once there the response was brilliant.

On reaching the Hospital, medic's came out and transferred the injured from the van, in a most caring and considerate way. Now me and Sev could only wait. Sev went inside to speak to the doctors who were attending to the riders. The guy who had been landed on, by most of the other riders had a fractured skull. John had a broken femur, the main bone in the thigh, and suspected head injuries and Pete Ralph had a shattered elbow. What a start to the trip this had been. The rider with the fractured skull was taken upstairs for an emergency operation and so was Pete but John was still in the trauma room having a quarter inch hole drilled through his knee joint, without anaesthetic, and a steel pin inserted through the hole. Wires were then attached to the pin with weights attached to the other end to put his leg in traction and try and pull the overlapping bones back into place. He was then taken upstairs to a recovery room.

Me and Sev got to see him about two hours later and as we entered the room John was lying on the bed with his injured leg being held in position by the wires and weights. In the next bed was Pete with his arm in a full plaster cast. It had been broken in seven places and it had literally been screwed back together again. John was still in shock and didn't really know the extent of his injuries. His doctor, Albert Lavrenov spoke some English and explained he had a clean break about four inches below the hip joint and it should heal OK so long as they could get both ends of the break to line up using the traction device. Normally this type of break would take about four months to heal satisfactorily.

John and Pete were both given sedatives to help them sleep so me and Sev left for the Planeta Hotel. All the other riders were there and keen to know how John and Pete were so we gave them all the information we had. I asked Sev why there had been no track marshals, first aid or medics at the practice session.

Sev went out to ring Ustymchuk and on his return he explained to me that the factory had a race organiser whose job it was to make sure everything was in place for the meeting and he was paid by the factory to do this job. It seems that because Saturday was only a practice day he had pocketed the money that should have been used to pay for the ambulances, medics and track marshals and he was now under arrest and being held in the Minsk Central Police Station, where on Monday morning, he would be charged with stealing the money. If a track marshal had been there on the brow of the hill the accident wouldn't have happened because, as the first rider came off in the dip he would have used his marshals flag and warned other riders coming up behind that there was an accident. This one guy, due to his greed, had jeopardised every rider.

It was decided to carry on with the actual race meeting on the Sunday and it was enjoyed by all our remaining riders. The results were: Lithuania won, with England second and Russia third and Belarus forth.

I left the meeting early with Sev to return to the hospital and on entering John's room was shocked to find his skin was turning dark. Pete said he had been watching John and was also concerned. He had noticed the change of skin colour and worsening condition. Sev sent a medic to find the doctor but he had just gone off duty so Sev summoned Albert Lavrenov, the trauma surgeon who initially saw John. When he entered the room he quickly examined John and then sent for a medical team who arrived within minutes. They expertly lifted the whole bed onto a set of wheels and transferred it, complete with John, to the Intensive Care Department.

Ten minutes later Dr. Albert came back to see us in the waiting room and Sev asked what was happening. Dr Albert explained that the situation was very grave, and they thought John had an embolism. Not knowing what this meant he went on to explain to us that marrow, seeping from the broken bone, was entering the blood stream where it was attacking the red blood cells and the condition was potentially fatal. I felt sick, I never imagined you could die from a broken leg, it just didn't seem possible. For goodness sake all he'd done was break his leg! I pulled myself together and asked Dr Albert what could be done for John. He said that personally he couldn't do anything, it was not his specialist area, but he had a friend who worked in the Ukraine Research Institute, and another friend at the Moscow State hospital and both had many years of studying this condition. He said he would ring them immediately and he left me and Sev to be escorted to the Intensive Care Department to see John, whose skin looked even blacker than before, and he was now unconscious.

The thought of being 3000 miles from home didn't help the situation. The Regent team were leaving on the Tuesday morning and I had a meeting with them all on the Monday afternoon to tell them of John's condition. They were all visibly shocked and upset at the news and after wishing them a safe journey back to England, me and Sev returned to the Hospital where a representative from a Swedish Hospital was waiting to see me. He said,

'If we fly your son to Sweden he will get better treatment than here in Russia.' I asked what it would cost to fly John and was told £25,000 to £30,000, payable up front before we move him.' Albert interrupted and said that the treatment John was getting was as good as he would get anywhere, and that he had already enquired about the possibility of John flying back to England for treatment, but had been told by his specialist friend that flying with an embolism would most certainly kill him, so it seems our Swedish friend was more interested in the money that could be made, than in the patient, so I politely told him to clear off.

Both of Albert's expert friends had booked flights to Minsk and would be here the next morning to help John. I had spoken to Val and explained the situation and she booked a flight to Moscow for Ellen, Johns wife while she stayed at home to look after their children and the business. Sev got a friend to meet Ellen at Moscow and bring her to Minsk and the factory had organised an emergency visa for her to enter Russia. They also organised accommodation for us both in a flat at a new complex.

Even before he arrived, the specialist had advised Albert to give John an emergency blood transfusion, which he did after checking John's blood group. The help everyone was giving was unbelievable, they felt it was a matter of pride that John should survive this accident.

The next morning as promised both specialists were at John's bedside discussing with Albert a plan of action in an attempt to save John's life. They had between them both over 30 years experience in dealing with embolism and the treatment of the condition. Albert said that if anybody could save John it was these two guys and for over a week they both stayed at the hospital, day and night, working full time on John.

Ellen arrived and was visibly shocked when she saw John's condition, he had pipes into his chest, his legs and arms. Everyday we left the flat, went straight to the hospital to see John and have a meeting with the specialists, and stayed with him for the rest of the day, then went back to the flat, to repeat it all over again the next day. On the ninth day after Ellen arrived John regained consciousness and his colour was improving, the heavy black tone of his skin was fading. We met both specialists in the corridor just outside the room and they confirmed that John had turned the corner. It's not often I embrace a doctor, or a specialist, one of each in this case, but I found myself hugging them both with joy at this news, even Albert got a big hug when he arrived. Ellen also hugged them all, and even Sev joined in the spontaneous hugging frenzy, and we all thanked them for their generous help in saving John's life. They told us that they thought he would be back to normal health in about three weeks but that his leg would take another two months for the bone to knit together. The Specialists had told Sev before they left that John had had an extra full blood transfusion and some special medication that Alex had brought with him from his research institute in Kiev, Ukraine.

Albert explained that such specialists were poorly paid in Russia and they had come to Minsk at their own expense. They personally had not asked for anything but Albert asked if I could help them by paying for their return journey. I happily gave them both $500 each, which considering they earned only $25 a week salary, was a lot of money to them. I never knew their full names but Alex from Ukraine and Uri from Moscow both appreciated the gesture as much as we appreciated their help.

John's condition was improving slowly every day. Pete had undergone further surgery and his arm was improving. Marty flew out from England to lend some moral support and help in any way he could with John's recovery so a week after his arrival I accompanied Pete back to the UK by train. We had been in Minsk for two months and there were arrangements to be made for John's return, hopefully in two or three weeks time. Val was obviously relieved and pleased at the outcome and my return. She said that the news of John's accident had spread after the return of the Regent MX team and the amount of people who rang Regent daily for news of John's progress was unbelievable, amounting to about 40 calls a day.

Eventually Ellen rang to say that Dr Albert thought John was now well enough to travel back to England, but that he thought it advisable to accompany John in order to monitor his condition. Val contacted British airways and tickets were booked for Albert, John and Ellen. John was in a full body cast up to his chest for travelling to make sure the barely set bones in his leg couldn't move. The first leg of the journey was by train, from Minsk to Moscow airport.

The big day finally arrived for John's return journey. Sev and Irena his wife said their goodbyes and a phone call from Ellen confirmed that John was to start his trip that night at about 6 pm from Minsk station. John lay on a stretcher unable to move because of his full length cast, so picture this. The sleeper carriage John was assigned, had stopped short of the platform, and the carriage door was a good six feet above ground level so the stretcher had to be slotted in the doorway at head height. While the stretcher was still only halfway onto the carriage the train started to slowly move out of the station, with John half in and half out of the doorway. As the train gathered speed, Ellen and Albert were inside frantically pulling and two guys were outside running alongside the carriage frantically pushing the stretcher with John hanging on for dear life. With a last major effort the stretcher was pushed inside and a difficult trip to Moscow Central Station followed.

On arrival there John was unloaded onto the platform. Val had contacted the Red Cross to transport John from the station to the airport by ambulance, but they refused to load him into the ambulance. When asked what the problem was, the driver said they wanted paying up front before they went anywhere. Ellen had to ring Val who organised an urgent bank transfer to the Red Cross in Moscow, but it took four hours to get there while John, Ellen, and Albert had to just wait. When eventually the transfer came through, they were all taken to the airport and were driven on to the airfield.

They were expected and customs cleared all the paperwork for the trip. Laying on his stretcher John looked up at the towering aircraft above and wondered how he was going to get up to the rear door of the aircraft. The answer soon became apparent as two airport workers, aged about 50, arrived with a stretcher chair. They propped John against it at an angle and strapped him to it and with much pushing and pulling dragged John up the plane steps, stopping several times to regain their breath. He said later that he often had nightmares about this.

They finally got him inside the plane but as John could only lay across the seats, the English Captain came out of the cockpit and told Ellen that she would have to take John off the aircraft as he was taking up too much room on the plane and was a danger to other passengers. Finally at the end of her tether Ellen burst into tears, but all the other passengers on board protested en mass. If the Captain refused to take John to the UK they would all boycott the plane. Eventually he relented and agreed to take John, but we were charged for 3 extra seats. Good old British Airways.

The only constructive, and freely given help we did get, was from the Barton upon Humber branch of the St John's Ambulance Service, who offered to go to the airport and collect John and transport him home in their ambulance and they asked for no payment, either up front or at all. This is how I found myself travelling down the A1 in an ambulance with two guys who did this as volunteer work.

John's plane had landed about half an hour before we arrived at the airport and as we entered the arrivals department John was being pushed out of the customs, on a stretcher with Ellen by his side and Albert pushing him. He was taken to the ambulance and transferred onto their own stretcher and then settled inside and the trip home began. I felt very grateful to these kind people who would accept nothing for themselves so I gave a donation of £250 to The St. Johns Ambulance Service plus I paid for the fuel to and from Heathrow.

It was late at night when we arrived back and a relieved Val and Wayne had a bed set up in the living room for John and a room ready for Albert. It was good to have John home and he had a constant stream of visitors, friends and business associates, from all over the country, including Neil Tuxworth, and many of the staff at Honda UK, Louth who came over to see him. After resting for four days Albert suggested that John should be taken to the hospital for x rays to check that the bones were still healing ok and had stayed inline.

Arrangements were made and John was taken to the Hull Royal Infirmary for these checks.

Albert had taken the trouble before leaving Russia to translate all John's notes into English and he took these with him to the hospital. To Albert's horror the doctors said they were going to remove the full body cast, as in the UK, they no longer used this old fashioned type of cast. Albert gave them the translated notes and x rays which were just casually dismissed and he was told.

'You're not in Russia now.' They then wheeled John off to another department in the hospital. He was brought back about an hour later without the body cast and all he had on his injured leg was a polycarbonate support going up to his groin. Albert protested loudly saying,

'The leg will not be sufficiently supported to hold in place, and the bone is likely to heal bent.' but the English doctors insisted they knew best. A month later on another visit, the x rays, to check the progress showed that Albert had been right, the bone was healing but was now over one inch out of line and with new callous growing between the V of the bend nothing more could be done. Now, thanks to the Hull

Royal Infirmary, John walks with a limp and has one leg shorter than the other. Albert had a meeting with the offending doctors and told them what he thought of their so-called superior expert knowledge. As a parting shot he asked them if they could have saved John's life when he had the embolism and looking at each other they all admitted that no, if he'd had an embolism with the broken femur they couldn't have saved him, he would probably have died.

'Russia 1, England 0.' was Albert's departing words to them.

Pete Ralph also had similar problems with the doctors at Hull Royal Infirmary who insisted that the pin in his elbow should stay in place, but it turned septic and expelled itself out of his arm making further surgery necessary.

Nev Mason
saying
1992
A totally positive attitude is the major thing that will advance you forward in life.

Me and John at the Minsk M/X track

Top: Minsk factory Director's lunch
Bottom: Minsk storage yard, filled and emptied daily

Top: Our RTX factory - inside Motovelo's factory
Bottom: 1st batch of RTX 125 Trials bikes

Chapter 15

John spent most of the year organising Stuart Coyle's world championship rides and running the shop, but we also designed and built a new trials bike range which was given the name RTX. The idea was to produce a new bike at a second hand price, a beginners bike that had the modern fork angle, rear foot rest position and was a twin shock. The first prototype was built in just three days and on the fourth day it was tested against a Yamaha TY 125 to compare it.

Our local trials expert, Colin Thomson, rated the RTX. He said it had better suspension, better steering, better balance and was far slimmer that the Yamaha TY 125, so on day five I was on my way to Belarus with the RTX stripped down to just the frame and swinging arm and a further four days after arriving at the Motovelo factory in Minsk we had the first pre production 125cc prototype finished and ready for testing. It underwent the full test procedure at the factory which took a month to complete and within two months we had, back in the UK, the first batch of ten sample bikes for evaluation and testing. Designing the fibreglass bodywork was done by John and Rob Margetson together.

The bike was to sell retail for £995 including vat. It was advertised in Trials and MX News and Motor Cycle News and we soon had a long waiting list with confirmed orders for it, not just from the UK but from France, Holland, Spain, Italy, Czechoslovakia, Estonia, Norway, Australia, Japan and the USA. My point had been proven, there was a big market for a low cost trials play bike and only four months after the first prototype was built the first production batch of 100, semi completed bikes, arrived at our base at Goxhill.

They were built up here in the UK at Goxhill, and were fitted as standard equipment with Pirelli trials tyres, Renthal alloy handlebars, Venhill UK cables, German ceramic clutch plates, Latvian Motoplat type electronic ignition, Kawasaki 125 foam air filter elements and a UK manufactured body kit and mudguards. When me and John set out to design this bike it was meant to be a Yamaha TY replacement, just a learner bike, and to be used as a weekend play bike, but what we didn't expect was that within a month of the RTX being launched we had customers ringing us up to inform us they had just won, on their RTX, a local trial they had entered just for fun, or they had just won the twin shock class at a trials meeting. Every week RTX125's were getting mentioned in the weekly bike papers results columns.

Many people were now asking for a bigger engine so I was back on the train to the factory in Minsk to develop a 212cc engine, which was the biggest capacity we could get out of this engine, without having to produce new crankcases to accommodate a bigger bore. It turned out only 16 BHP at 4000 revs, but that was enough to start with. On the next batch of 125cc bikes, we added 3 inches to the carb inlet casting length and 9ins to the front exhaust length, both to improve the bottom end pulling power, and with the new type, slightly heavier flywheels, the primary gearing was also lowered making it even more suitable for the none expert rider.

I have seen what happens when you put a novice rider on a trials bike with a quick response, high revving engine, with a very responsive power band, they either flip upside down or slide all over the place, as the power kicks in. With the RTX they just opened the throttle and went, without losing control because of the flat spread of the power delivery of the bike.

That's just what it was designed to do. The reason we used the Minsk engine was because we had dealt with this factory for over 20 years and although it was not the most sophisticated engine in the world it was time proven and very reliable, plus it had a cassette gearbox and was very easy to work on, and spares were readily available and cheap to buy. Our Neval and Regent road bikes used an earlier side exhaust port version of this engine.

We made the decision to concentrate on the manufacturing and distribution of our RTX bikes worldwide, so we sold our retail motocross shop to Rob Margetson who lived in Barrow, just down the road from us and I bought a big farm at North Killingholme, about four miles away. It had been a dairy farm, had 10 acres of land a large farm house and many big sheds and out buildings which would be ideal to use for manufacturing and assembling bikes in.

Church Farm, as it was called, was on the market for £110,000 but I managed to buy it for £95000, as the farm house needed a complete renovation which took us six months to complete, before everything was then moved to our new home at the year end.

Church Farm - we bought at Killingholme

Top: The house that overlooks the river Humber
Bottom: The big house on the hill we bought at South Ferriby

Over the next year we slowly increased the production of the RTX trials bikes and increased the size of our workforce in the Belarus factory. We doubled the manufacturing area in our allotted part of the factory, plus we had the pick of the best workers for our department. Our workers were paid more than the normal factory floor worker so we always had a waiting list of skilled technicians hoping to get on to the RTX project. The management at the factory was very strong at this time, they had to be because the factory Mafia was constantly trying to expand their empire inside the plant and it seemed to me that while the Communist system was in power the Mafia was held at bay.

Our production was now averaging about 100 RTX a month, all RTX T125's. Later that year the first batch of 50, RTX T 212 twin shocks were made. We exhibited the RTX bikes at the German, Cologne International Show, where we certainly got a far bigger response than we expected. We even had some guys from two of the big Japanese manufacturers looking all over the bikes and taking photos.

It was in January 1993, while driving through South Ferriby, a quaint hillside village overlooking the

River Humber, near Barton, when I spotted a very large, fairly new house built into the hillside with a for sale sign on it. I pulled to a stop then drove up the steep driveway to the house. When you stood with your back to the house the views were amazing. The urge to own and live in this house was overwhelming and within ten minutes I was at the agents office in Barton to find out all I could about it.

The house had been built by a local builder for a Barton businessman who lived in it for only a few years before going bust. There were three banks involved and the asking price was £112,000 being an impulse buyer, I offered them £90,000 for it. They consulted the banks and I was surprised when the offer was accepted. I contacted my solicitor to get things going. At this point I had not said anything to Val or John about the house.

A week later I got a phone call from the estate agent to say that all the banks had had a rethink and had instructed the agent to have a sealed bid auction for the house, so I upped my offer to £100,000 but this was rejected and I was told I must send in a sealed offer by the following Friday. I didn't like their tactics so didn't bother to send an offer to them, I had lost interest in it and was pleased I had not yet mentioned it to the family, and put it out of my mind.

The Monday following the auction day, I got a phone call from the agent saying they were surprised I had not sent in an offer for the house, so I told them that I had no intention of getting into a bidding war. They explained that they had not received a bid higher than the £100,000 so they had been instructed to accept that offer.

'It's my original bid of £90,000 that I'll stand by.'

'But you said you would give £100,000 for it.'

'That was before you tried to con me into an imaginary sealed bidding war. It's £90,000 take it or leave it.' I said and put down the phone on Mr Smart Alex. Two weeks passed without any contact then I received a letter from the bank's agent saying they had decided to accept my offer of £90,000 for the house. I sent a letter back to them enclosing a bill for £206 which I had received from my solicitor for the aborted sale and told them if they agreed to pay it, the sale of the house would be back on, if not, forget it. They agreed to pay the bill and forwarded all the relevant paperwork regarding the sale of the house to my solicitors.

As it was now looking like it would go through I took Val and John to see the house on the hill I had first seen weeks earlier. I asked them what they thought about living here. They both looked dumb struck, the house had cost a fortune to build and was only seven years old. Val looked through the window into the kitchen .

'It's beautiful, it must have cost a fortune to fit it out like that.' John nodded his agreement.

'Well what do you think?' I asked them both 'because it's make your mind up time, I've already bought it, it's going through the solicitors right now.'

'Why haven't you told us about it before now?' they wanted to know.

'It was meant to be a secret.' I said. 'A surprise.'

'Do you mean you have bought it without even going inside?' Val asked.

'I didn't need to, it's only six years old and you can see the standard it's built to just looking through the windows, why would I need to go inside for a look, besides, turn round and look at that view.' On the way home Val was deep in thought.

'You don't think people will say we're trying to be posh, do you?' she muttered.

View of the Humber bridge

View from the big house overlooking the Humber

'They can say what they like.' I said. 'Would you both rather live there or Church Farm?' They looked at each other then came back with a resounding.

'You're right, there's no comparison, it will be much better to live there than Church Farm.' The house was fantastic but the beautiful elevated view over the river Humber was what sealed it. It looked like we were moving yet again As soon as the sale was completed I collected the keys and we all went inside for the first time.

The house was three stories high and as we had seen through the windows fitted out to a very high standard. The full ground floor area was a colossal self contained annex apartment which me and Val claimed as our home and John and Debbie settled on floor two for John and his family and the top floor for Debbie and her family. Everybody stood looking out of the panoramic windows at the view which went right across the River Humber to the north bank, this really was a view to die for. Wayne stayed at the new house for a few days to look after the place until me and Val completed our move but it became apparent we didn't have enough furniture to fill the place. It was so much bigger than we thought it was going to be. The front room was so big we had to buy three new ten foot long settees just to fill the room out plus a new big dining table and chair set and two massive coffee tables and we added a new TV as our old one looked like a small dot in the distance. A new king sized bed completed that afternoons buying spree.

Anecdote

Sitting looking out of the widow of the new flat the Minsk factory bosses had acquired for me and Ellen, John's wife, to stay in while John was in hospital in Minsk I watched as a large open truck pulled up outside the department store opposite. It was full of brand new steel wheelbarrows. It was twenty below zero and about two feet deep in snow when they unloaded all the wheelbarrows onto the side of the road. I watched in sheer amazement as people came running from all directions. They piled the wheelbarrows up to ten high then paid for them before hurrying off up the road with them. When Sev arrived to drive us to the hospital I asked why these people had wanted so many wheelbarrows each? **'They just buy them to sell Nev.'**

Chapter 16

Within a week of being in our new home an urgent phone call came from Sev at the factory. The RTX production had come to a stop, with only five days to go before they were due to load the next RTX shipment into the two 40 foot containers for shipping them to us in the UK. It seems the factory owed a mere $400000 for an unpaid electricity bill, so their supply had been cut off.

'What do you want me to do Sev, pay the bill for them?' a quiet laugh came back over the phone.

'No Nev but if you are here perhaps you can find a way of solving our problem.'

The next day I was on the train in Holland yet again on my way to Minsk. The trip takes just under two days and when I finally arrived in Minsk a car was waiting to pick me up from the station and take me to Sev's office where we both sat in the dark unlit room talking.

Sev told me that the whole factory had been cut off now for four days. I asked him if the Bear and the Weasel were still the joint heads of the factory Mafia.

'Yes they are but why do you ask me this

question?' '

'I seem to remember Sev, that the Weasel claimed he has contacts with the local Army Commandant. Can you ring the Weasel now and ask him over here?' Five minutes later in walked the very appropriately named person and Sev asked if he did indeed still have his contacts with the Army Commandant.

'Yes Nev he says he does.'

'Then ask him if he can borrow a large Army generator from him, it will earn both of them some money.' The word money got an instant reaction from him and he disappeared from the room. An hour passed before he returned.

'Where do you want it? Shall I take it to the RTX building?' Me and Sev got up and looked out of the window where a massive generator was sat on the back of a large six wheeled Army Kamaz truck parked outside. We went out and got into the truck and gave the driver the directions to our RTX building and soon our bit of the factory was the only part of the plant that had electricity and was working. It cost me $500 but it got the next RTX shipment finished and ready to leave on time.

Top: Water cooled Minsk racing engines
Bottom: Russian build world championship kart

Top: Russian kart with Minsk engine
Bottom: Our kart track

I stayed on for a week as Sasha, the guy who worked for me part time, translating and sourcing products, was due back from Moscow where he had been tracking down a factory that produced go karts fitted with Minsk engines. When he came back he was very excited. He had found the Go Kart producing factory and had made an appointment for us to visit the next day. Another overnight train journey saw us both waiting on the Moscow train station platform for transport from the kart factory to collect us. The Russians are not the best time keepers in the world and the car arrived only an hour late but on our arrival at the factory we were taken straight to the dining room where we were given breakfast. During this meal we were introduced to the Director .

The kart plant was very large, covering approximately 15 acres and produced between 400,000 to 500,000 karts a year for distribution throughout Russia. They had a test track at the back of the factory where we were given a demonstration of the karts capabilities and I must admit to being surprised and impressed to see the karts with tuned, Minsk engines, doing about 85 m.p.h. top speed, and even more surprised when they wheeled out two special GP karts both fitted with water cooled Minsk 125 super tuned engines, which ran at about 115 m.p.h. top speed.

There were three classes of Karts they used the Minsk Engines in. The standard engine class, the tuned engine class, and the super tuned engine class. Offered a test ride round the track I couldn't believe just how quick they went, even pulling my weight, I was about 17 stone at that time. They said, via Sash, that they needed a week to work out some export prices for me, so we travelled over night again back to Minsk.

Sash asked if he could have the day off as he had not seen his family for 6 days, due to going backwards and forwards to Moscow. He planned to take his wife and kids to see a big open air Rock concert that was being held and televised in the main square in Minsk and asked if I would like to go with them. I like most types of music so readily agreed.

The concert that evening lasted approximately four hours and there were two bands that stood out from all the rest. A group called Krama and one called Tornado, a name I seemed to think was already being used by a group on the western music scene. After the concert I was introduced to all the members of Krama, which it seemed was amongst the top Belarus pop

Top: Members of our top Russian group Krama
Bottom: Debut Krama album I produced

Two of the Russian rock albums we released

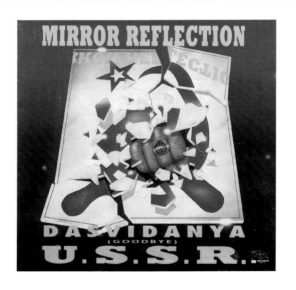

groups, with regular TV and radio spots. I was also given demo tapes which I brought back with me to the UK and this was to be the start of my involvement in the music business. The groups could not speak or sing in English but the music was as good as anything I had heard in the west.

Sev rang on the night I returned home to say that the factory had had its electricity bill paid by the Belarus Government. Well, he said they had paid half the total bill, and the electricity company was told to clear off and forget the rest of the money, but the factory was now working 24/7 to catch up with all their back orders.

The Kart factory had finally contacted Sash and given him some export prices which he faxed through to me, but unknown to the factory or to Sash, Sev had got hold of their latest export prices to Sweden, and these were approximately thirty five percent cheaper than the prices they had given to Sash, so I told Sev to tell them I would be back in Russia in about four weeks time and would call and see them then.

In the four weeks I was back in the UK, me and John built a new model, disc braked, mono shocked prototype trials bike, which we gave the name RTX

MD 212. We fitted a 28mm carb instead of 24mm and a new type of silencer. It looked well and, the engine revved a lot more, but we came to the conclusion it needed the compression raising a bit, so the cylinder head was machined off by 1 mm and what a difference it made. As well as pulling, it now had a bit of a kick in the motor but it was getting some clutch slip when under load, but fitting stronger clutch springs solved this problem.

Colin Thomson took it out round his own trials test track over the weekend and gave it a good working over. Trials and Moto Cross News ran a test article on the twin shock RTX T125 and the new mono disc RTX MD 212 and their reporters gave both bikes an excellent test report, but said they both preferred, of the two models, the twin shock RTX T125. It just goes to show you can't please everybody. Then, in May 1995, the monthly magazine, Dirt Bike Rider, did a full test session on the RTX 125 Trials bike. The test rider was none other than Steve Saunders, 10 times British Trials Champion, who said;

'For the money, the RTX 125 has just got to be a brilliant trials bike.' He also said. 'The overall riding position, balance and feel of the bike, is good and quite

You don't need a big wad to go trials riding, as Steve Saunders finds with the new budget-priced but big performing bikes from RTX.

"For the money, the RTX125 has just got to be a brilliant trials bike." Who says so? Only DBR's resident test pilot, 10 times British Champion Steve Saunders after an afternoon on a couple of the new budget - mega-low-budget actually - trials bikes. "OK, they're not perfect and I'll point out the faults later, but they make excellent starter-bikes. Let me put it this way, I've ridden plenty of TY175 Yamahas that performed a lot worse than this," said Steve.

So, what is an RTX? The RTX took shape in

Main picture: For the money, the RTX 125 Twinshock, is excellent value and an ideal entry-level machine for newcomers or novices.
Left: Something for everyone; from left: the RTX 125 Twinshock, the Monodisc M212 prototype and the Twinshock 212.

the mind of North Eastern entrepreneur Nev Mason after he got fed-up with lads coming into his Regent Motocross shop in Hull asking for cheap trials bikes to play on. His stock of old TY175 Yams was exhausted so he thought 'Why not build a replacement?'

"I have had business contacts in Eastern Europe - don't call it Russia - for over 20 years and can get anything made in a huge motorcycle factory in Belarus." Don't head for the Atlas, it is one of the new Baltic States, like Latvia and Estonia - "so it was a relatively easy venture for me.

"You have got to understand, this was never meant to be a serious trials bike, just something for lads (grown up lads as well) to learn to ride on and to play on at weekends. I designed and built the prototype myself in January 1993, took it to the factory and the first 20 production bikes were delivered to me in April! That is how fast they can react to orders.

"I designed the RTX to be utterly simple and totally bullet-proof," says Nev.

The two-stroke piston- ported engine is basically a 125cc design with the porting bearing a remarkable similarity with a TY Yam. A German-sourced crank drives a clutch via a Maico primary drive chain and the power is then transmitted through a four-speed box ◀

Left: The test RTX 212 came fitted with a prototype disc. The engine was very tight for the test so most of the riding was done on the 125.

Below: Parts are sourced wherever quality and price match. The head and barrel come from Belarus, the crank and clutch from Germany, the ignition from Latvia and the Mikuni carburettor from India.

"I spent a long time - mainly on the 125 - this afternoon and for £1200 it has to be a cracking little bike. The engine starts dead easy and really is a little belter. It thrives on revs of course but it is also quite torquey." - SAUNDERS.

Test done by Steve Saunders
on RTX Trials bike

Top: 1st RTX Mono Disc 220cc
Bottom: 1st RTX 125cc Twin Shock

modern and I like the totally neutral steering, which is very important for beginners and novices, and the twin shock rear suspension works well.' Steve Saunders conclusions were,

'For the money the RTX 125 Twin shock is excellent value and an ideal entry level machine for newcomers and novices. I spent a long time, mainly on the 125 this afternoon,' he said, 'and for just under £1200 new, it has to be a cracking little bike. The engine starts easily and it really is a little belter. It thrives on revs of course, but it is also quite torquey.'

John Dickinson, the Editor of Trials and Motocross News also tested an RTX in a National Twin shock round at Fell Green, Bootle in 1995 and said he was pleased with his 24 mile, moorland ride on it.

It was very nice to see in the veteran trials journalist, Don Morley's full page test report on our RTX twin shock trials bikes that he really rated them. The RTX bikes handling, suspension and balance at such a low price amazed him and his quote was; 'The RTX boys have worked wonders on the bikes rear suspension, it's excellent.' Not too bad for a bike that took me and John only three days to conceive, build and finalise the testing of the first prototype bike. It took just less than three months to get this bike into full production. The first batch of our 125cc RTX trials bikes were winning trials events within weeks of the first shipment arriving ready to be assembled here in the UK. Trials and Moto Cross News also did a full page test on our RTX trials bikes by Sean Lawless and Mike Rapley and they both rated the RTX very highly. **A Quote from their full length test was; 'A quick test ride is all it takes to silence any critics who contend that it's impossible to produce a completive trials bike at such a low cost. It's a superb bargain.'**

Chapter 17

I was playing the Krama and Tornado demo tapes to many of the local music experts around our area and they all agreed the music was quite good.

A guy called Chris McRae from Grimsby, who was a local record producer, listened to the Belarus band's demo tapes and thought the potential was good. His preference was for Tornado who were a great sounding thrash metal band lead by Angus, a real character, a 27 year old whose father, an army captain, had him locked up in prison for 2 years because he played in a rock band and had long hair. McRae made the fatal mistake of saying he would like to meet them, so I told him.

'It's no problem. I'm going back over to Belarus in two weeks you can come with me if you want and see them play for yourself.' So two weeks later me and Chris were at London Airport catching a plane to Lithuania. I had been assured by a friend that Lithuanian planes were quite safe as they were American made Boeings, and I must admit it was one of the better flights I have ever experienced. The plane arrived at the airport at 6 30pm and at 9 pm there was no sign of Sash who was supposed to be picking us up at 7 pm. Time passed and at 10 pm, over the tannoy system, there was a call for Mr Nev Mason to go to doorway three where a smiling Sash was waiting with what looked like a carbon copy of that great hairy thing in Star Wars, Chewbacca.

It was pitch black outside as we felt our way across to an ancient red Moskovitch parked up under the only car park light that was working. At this point in time Lithuania, Latvia and Estonia had broken away from Russia, so to cross the border into Belarus it just cost one dollar for each of us for the guards back pockets. Chris seemed to be quite afraid of the guards who were walking around the car toting AK47 Machine Guns but I told him not to worry, after all my years of being in Russia I was used to the sight of guns being carried, it was quite normal.

We finally got to Minsk at 2.30am. Sash had booked us into a private apartment which belonged to one of the band member's parents, and was next door to the apartment they lived in, and I'm sure they didn't appreciate the noise of our late arrival as it drifted through the dividing wall. Chewbacca lived in the apartment directly above ours, it felt a lot safer, Chris said, knowing that he was close by.

As the sun came up all the local frogs in the area began calling out to their mates across the other side of the river which was opposite our apartment, what a racket they made. Sash arrived, he had arranged breakfast at a nearby café, and in the middle of the meal something brushed past my leg, thinking it was a pet cat I looked down at the floor and froze.

'Sash, look Sash,' I pointed to a large fat rat that was now sat under our table eating some leftovers.

'What's the problem Nev, don't you like rats?'

'Not when they are in a so called café, and when I'm eating food, I don't.' the Rat moved off to the next table, luckily unseen by Chris.

Over the next two days we auditioned about 10 groups in Minsk, then went on to Mozyr, a town which had a modern recording studio, owned by the group, Mirror Reflection, who were sponsored by a large American backed, Russian oil company. The studio was full of top of the range equipment which Chris found very difficult to use as his equipment in Grimsby was very old hat compared to this gear. He took me to one side and said.

'I can't record Krama, I don't know how to use this gear at all. It's just too high tech for me.'

'Look Chris, we're 3000 miles from home, our return tickets are not for another 12 days, so just go back in there and bluff it out. Ask them to run you through how to use all their equipment. Tell them it's a bit out dated compared to what you're used to in England.' two hours later a now smiling Chris came out of the sound track room after two of the top guys in Mirror Reflection had shown him how everything worked.

It was now our intention to record Krama's album, all 10 tracks, using English vocals. We started 7 days of continuous recording work, 14 hours a day, teaching Krama, but particularly Igor the lead singer, how to sing in English, in a Yorkshire cum Lincolnshire accent. Bit by bit we finally got there. We had 9 tracks recorded and then ran out of time. We were doing the basic recording onto master tapes at the Mozyr studio and all the mixing was going to be done in England. We altered some of the lyrics on several tracks to make them flow better. I wouldn't have thought it was possible to teach Russians, who didn't speak any English, track by track all the vocals well enough to record them.

Mixed and produced in the UK, Krama's, and

Belarus' first ever CD, which I titled 'Vodka on Ice' received much acclaim when finished. It was mixed at Fairview studios in Anlaby, by John Spence, a well known and respected figure in the music industry in the UK. On the last day before we left Mozyr we recorded Mirror Reflections album in English. They already spoke English but with an American accent. Tornado, lead by Angus, sang one of their tracks called 'We Are Dynamite'

I explained to Angus that the name Tornado was already used by another group in the west so they would have to think of another name, but how about Red Dynamite was my suggestion. They leapt up and down in excitement, they thought it was a brilliant name for them. Angus could already speak good English so they could record their album at Mozyr without us being there. They completed the work then couriered the master tape to us in England by DHL, but unfortunately DHL managed to lose the tape and it all had to be done again.

Before returning to the UK I managed to get two days working in our dept in the Motovelo factory, and me and Sev began organising a small, first production batch of RTX Mono Disc 212 but because we wanted to change the swinging arm fitment to take a single shock instead of the normal twin shock arrangement and have a new front hub in alloy cast up for the disc brake, we had to go and see the Bear and the Weasel, as their dept controlled all the changes to the standard production items. The Bear stood about six foot six and must have weighed about 24 stone with a large bushy beard. His Mafia partner in their department, the Weasel, stood about five foot 2in and weighed about 7 stone, both were very appropriately named.

Unfortunately, to get things done in this factory, a Mafia contribution had to be paid to these two despots, and in this case they demanded $2000 before they would authorise the work to be started for the MD 212 project. I told them to get stuffed, $1000 was as much as I was prepared to pay them. The weasel opened his office desk drawer and took out a really nice presentation box, passing it across to me, he asked me to reconsider my offer. Sev indicated that it was time to leave their office and later, back in Sevs apartment just before his wife Irena put out tea, I thought I would look at the unexpected present they had given me. Opening the smart, sealed box, I looked at the contents, a ceremonial dagger and a square rubber ink eraser. Sevs face had a look of horror on it.

'What's all this about Sev?' I asked him.

'It's a threat Nev, it's a way of them saying to you they can eliminate you.'

'Then what's the best way to handle them?' I asked. Sev rang somebody who advised us to give the present back to them, indicating we were not afraid of them, so the next day I returned to their department and, presented it back to them. They both looked rather worried by this action, I don't think they had ever had one of their presents returned to them before. Sev translating for me told them.

'Nev says he has worked in Russia for over 20 years and he's still here, he says that if anything happens to him he will give both of you a guarantee now, that within one day, the same thing will happen to both of you.' We turned and left, Sev was looking even more nervous than before we went to see them.

'Nev I'm worried they will cause problems for you.'

'Don't worry Sev I've got this to help protect me when I am in Russia.' Opening my wooden brief case, which went everywhere with me, I pulled out a small black resin box with a button on top, it's the first time

I ever saw Sev lost for words.

'We call it an emergency button.' he replied 'how did you get that?'

'A guy at Avtoexport gave it to me years ago and told me if ever I had serious trouble in Russia all I had to do was press the button and a protector would be with me within a few minutes to help me. He had explained to me that there were a lot of people in Russia who do not like Westerners being in their country.'

'Perhaps I should tell the Mafia pair you have the emergency button protection.' He must have said something to them as the price for the T212 project changed and suddenly dropped to $1000 and after this I never had any more trouble.

On the journey back to Lithuania the next day to catch the plane home, we got Chewbacca and his famous world championship Moskovich rally car again, which now had the addition of a bright yellow stripe painted down each side of it (how cool was that). After an unbelievably quick journey both me and Chris were glad to finally get onto the plane, and eventually, back in England boarded the train for home. I took the master tapes of Paradox and White Stream X to John

Spence at Fairview Studios and left them with him to mix as he thought fit and went home where an order had just come in from the Seychelles for 8 RTX T125 sample trials bikes.

The demand for the RTX bikes was now starting to increase beyond what we were producing a month, so we had to up the production by 10 percent to just keep on top, but Sev was very good at organizing our department at the plant.

LESSONS IN LIFE

I once had a compelling gut feeling that the airplane we were about to catch in Russia was going to crash. I absolutely refused to fly on that plane and found out later that it did indeed crash, so always follow your instincts.

Nev Mason
saying
1994
Success is all a matter of just how much personal effort you are prepared to put in

Anecdote

I always found that most people in the world were just great to work and get on with.

We had a visit in England from some high up Dnieper factory bosses to look at the way we worked. All of them said they had been dreading their visit to us in England and when I asked why they answered,

'Because we are told in Russia that England is a country still living in World War Two conditions, and that you have very little food to eat here. So far what has amazed us are the many big shops we have seen with our own eyes which are full of food and goods to buy. Also we are told that everybody in England rides about on pushbikes because there are very few cars here. But now we know this is not true as we have seen for ourselves since we arrived that there are more cars here than in the whole of the Ukraine.'

Chapter 18

Out of the blue, a phone call came in from Czechoslovakia, asking if we were interested in buying 140 brand new CZ motocross bikes, both 400cc and 250cc, and all the latest models. It seems this guy had remembered seeing the Regent MX name on Stuart Coyles shirt at the Czechoslovakian GP and had tracked us down in England from this.

The bikes were destined for Russia and were already at the border, loaded on two lorries, but had been detained there waiting for confirmation of payment before crossing into Russia. There was internal turmoil in Russia as the Government had started to collapse and the department that normally paid for the bikes was not answering their phones, in fact, they said the lines were dead. We said that we would be interested in buying them, but how much did they want for each bike? The line went quiet, then we were told that the Russians give $180 for each bike, 400cc or 250cc, the same price. A quick tot up showed it totalled $25,200 I asked what the delivery costs to England would be and was told it would be a total of $25,600 for all the 140 CZ bikes, delivered to us in

England, and that it would take them two days to get to us. He was correct, two days later, two 40 foot artic units full of new CZ motocross bikes still in their boxes rolled into our yard. They looked a hell of a buy for $180 each, and we sold them all in just over 7 months.

About seven months after this shipment he rang again. This time they had found in a warehouse at Brest, on the border, 50 new CZ motocross bikes, 380cc and 250cc, the same models as the last shipment. This time, we were too busy with our RTX project so I rang Bill Brown at Wulfsport in Cumbria, to ask him if he was interested in buying them. I owed Bill a favour, so I put him straight onto the guy in Czechoslovakia so he could deal direct with him, and he got them at the same price as far as I know. They were delivered directly to him in Cumbria.

The RTX had now been in production for about 18 months and as standard equipment we fitted Pirelli tyres and tubes, Renthal alloy trials handlebars and Venhill cables all round, but we decided to stop fitting these components as standard because of big price rises in all these parts. We didn't want to have to raise the price of the bike, and most of the buyers of the trials starter bikes didn't really appreciate the difference between a Pirelli tyre or a less well know brand or alloy handlebars compared to steel handlebars. Customers were offered the branded parts as extras if they wanted them, but in the next six years of production of the RTX, we only sold seven sets of Pirelli's and five Renthal bars, so our decision not to fit them as standard on the bikes was the right one.

Around this time we were looking at the 50cc kids bike market which was dominated in the UK by Malaguti and Italjet. What we had noticed at our local practice tracks was that Dad always had to have a few laps round the track on the kid's bike just to show the kid how it should be done. As these bikes were built for kids they weren't really up to pulling a 16 stone Dad around the track and often broke the suspension. What was required, we thought, was a bike small enough for kids but strong enough to carry a full sized adult if required.

Looking for a basic machine to start off with I tracked down a moped factory in Latvia, which used to make a million road mopeds a year for the Russian market. Me, John and Wayne flew out to the factory where only a small part of the plant was still working, as 85% of their production and sales, which had been destined for the Russian market, had been lost when Latvia pulled out of the Soviet Union and became independent.

We had a good look round the basic road moped which was conveniently fitted with 10 inch wheels and from this John drew a few quick sketches to show them the direction we were looking at. An hour later me and John, with Wayne helping were working in their unheated workshop, at 20 degrees below freezing, knocking up prototypes from their standard road moped. In three freezing cold hours we had two prototype kids bikes sat on the workbench, but it was so cold, twice Wayne's hands had frozen to the hacksaw he was using and they had to be freed by using warm water.

I gave the factory a provisional order for 1000 of the new bikes, providing they sent by airfreight two acceptable, pre production samples within one week. They actually arrived at the airport in the UK three days after we arrived back.

Earlier in the year we had bought a 22 acre disused airfield at Elsham for future development but with 4 miles of runways it was great for testing bikes on. For over a month me, John and Wayne hammered

Me and Val playing on the beach in Southern Ireland

Yet more testing on our airfield
Top: Me and Jade   Bottom: Anatol and John

the new prototype kids bikes around the airfield, on both the tarmac track and the off road track we had made, and apart from a few modifications they both came through all the testing with no problems, either mechanically or on the frame components.

We were testing two types of 50cc engines. The first had a two speed, manual gearbox with gear lever, and manual clutch, the second, a single speed automatic gearbox. I rang the factory and asked them if they could send Sergei, the chief designer over to us so we could brief him on the modifications for the production bikes. No visas were needed to enter the UK from Latvia so he arrived the next day, and we spent the day after that on our airfield, doing all the final testing of the bikes with him. The final specifications were agreed between us, and I telephoned the Director to give him our order for 600, of the two speed model and 400 of the automatic single speed model.

The bikes were to be supplied to us without tyres fitted. We would fit them here in the UK, giving the customer the choice of having Dunlop motocross tyres or road type tyres fitted, on purchase of the bike. The names we gave these mini kids bikes was Dirt Monkey and Moto Monkey and they really were strong enough to carry full sized adults. The last two hours of testing on the airfield was done with John, Pete my brother and Wayne, a total combined weight of 41 stone, all piled onto the same little bike, nobody could dispute that our mini bikes were not strong enough for the job.

A public road ran along the side of the airfield and many cars were stopping, and people getting out, to watch in amazement, three adults all sitting on one small mini bike, and riding it around the airfield. They didn't know we were doing the ultimate destruction test on it. Perhaps they thought they were rehearsing for a circus act. Sergei was so impressed with this demonstration he took some photos to take back to Latvia to show the staff at the factory our unusual testing methods.

An interesting trend developed. About a week or so after we sold a bike, Dad, having found that he could ride it around without breaking anything, would order one for himself so he could ride around with the kids, Even Mums started to get in on the act. If Dad could have a mini bike to ride about on why couldn't she. Our Dirt Monkey two speed manual was in production for three years until the factory in Lithuania producing this

Top: 1st Prototype Tokoya 50 kids trials bike we made
Bottom Left: Testing 50cc kids Dirt Monkey, carrying
40 st in weight. Bottom Right: Brother Pete

Top: Original Dirt Monkey two speed
Bottom: Original Moto Monkey automatic

Top: 1st Prototype Champ TJ50 Trials
Bottom: 1st Prototype Champ Paddock Monkey

Top: 1st Prototype Champ MX50
Bottom: 1st Prototype Champ MX60

engine went bankrupt, so for a further year of production we used the single speed automatic engine from Jawa in Czechoslovakia, then they went kaput as well. In that four year period we sold just over 7000 two speed manual Dirt Monkeys and 2400 single speed automatic Moto Monkeys.

Alongside the Dirt and Moto Monkey, Adult/Kids bikes, we also designed, developed and built a new range of bikes just for kids. The Champ SX 50 Range, powered by a cracking little automatic engine built in St Petersburg, these bikes were in production for four years, and we sold a lot of them, We heard that Monto Motors in India was building the Italian Garelli 50cc automatic engine under license in India. We had experience of Monto Motors as we had been using their Pacco carburettors which they made under license from the Japanese firm Mikuni. These carburettors were used on the RTX project from the very start, in fact, they were so good even the Minsk factory started using them on all their engines. I sent Monto a fax asking for details on the 50cc Garelli engine and they told me they would be exhibiting at the Munich show in Germany in three weeks time and could we meet them on their stand there. This was no problem to us as we were also exhibiting at the Munich show with our RTX and Champ ranges.

Leaving Wayne to look after the stand for an hour or so me and John went over to the Monto Motors stand to meet them, only to find that they had gone to our stand to meet us. Wayne explained we had gone to their stand so they quickly returned and we talked with them for about an hour. They said they could supply us with the 50cc Garelli moped engines, with a one years parts warranty, at a price of £34 each delivered to England. They had a sample of this engine at the show and it looked very well made and it was agreed they would give us this engine at the end of the show to take back to the UK to test. On the last day of the show they arrived at our stand with two engines, the sample one we had seen and one they had removed from a moped so we had a second engine for testing. They declined any payment for these engines saying that it would be payment enough for them, if after testing, we decided to use their engines

When we returned back home from the show, the Monto Garelli engines were fitted into two of our old Dirt Monkey demonstration bikes and then taken out to our airfield for testing. I remember that day being very long, as we put in as many hours as possible, continuously hammering the bikes around the tracks, and after 6 hours we were all finally fed up of going round and round. The Garelli engines had outlasted us that day and given no problems at all, in fact they both went better as the day went on, and they freed off. The next afternoon we repeated the same testing procedure on the tracks but after 5 hours of riding everybody had had their fill and just wanted to go home for tea.

Now it was time to ring Monto. At the Munich Show we had seen on their stand a small moped that was fitted with 10 inch wheels which we thought would be ideal for down sizing to a mini bike, using the same concept as before, making it strong enough to carry a full sized adult without anything breaking. They agreed to air freight a sample moped to us so we could cut it down to the size we required.

It arrived 4 days later and was put into our workshop to be stripped down and modified and what we finished up with, out of the cut down road moped, was a really good little kids bike which was all totally in proportion.

We used the top frame tube as the petrol tank

and John designed the worlds first flat pack, plastic with a memory, full body kit for this new mini bike. We converted the engine to pull start, instead of the standard pedal start that was fitted to this engine. The finished bike, complete but without the new type of bodywork, was then air freighted back to the Monto factory in India for them to copy.

When the final production version of our bike was air freighted back to us we spent a week on testing the bike around the airfield. It had 17 hours of testing that week and apart from adjusting the back chain nothing else was required to keep it going, apart from petrol of course. All this had taken 4 weeks from first testing the engines to testing the finished bike. I rang Chand Mehter the owner of Monto Motors and discussed prices with him and within 10 minutes we had agreed a price for the full bike less the plastic bodywork, which would be fitted in our workshops in England.

The first order was for 1000 mini bikes built to the same specification as the sample bike we sent them, all to be delivered to England within ten weeks. They arrived here in 12 weeks, but only because the ship was delayed in Germany. They had managed to

Top: 1st Prototype Champ SX50 with Garelli engine
Bottom: 1st Prototype Champ SX55

Top: 1st Prototype Champ SX60
Bottom: 1st Prototype Champ 50 Quad

get only 160 bikes into a 40 foot container, which was not good enough, as it made the shipping costs too expensive. John studied the packing situation and managed to reduce the box size by fifty percent, which meant they would get 320 bikes into a 40 foot container, making them more cost efficient. By the fourth container John had redesigned the boxes yet again and now managed to get 380 bikes into a 40 foot container.

This new mini bike was added to our range of other Champ bikes, which were a result of a visit by John and Ellen, a few years before, to the Chinese factories of Lifan, Kinroad and Zongshen to see if we could interest them in making off road fun bikes for us.

All these factories were interested in this new leisure fun bike sector. None of them had spotted this large, worldwide, off road market. Lifan showed the most interest so John showed them what was required and left a prototype of a modified road bike he had converted to a 125cc, two stroke, off road fun bike for them, plus a 50cc four stroke, off road, Dirt Cross. Samples arrived in England within one month of John and Ellen's visit to the Chinese, Lifan Factory. It would seem we had kick started the Chinese off road fun bike revolution.

This was the start of our involvement with the Chinese motorcycle producing factories and the off road fun bike market is now one of China's biggest exports of motorcycles, and all the factories, big or small, make and sell them throughout the world. Our involvement with the Chinese factories continued to evolve . We used our time proven method of making a prototype, testing it and if everything was ok then air freighting it back to the factory for them to copy. We now had a full range of Champ brand motorcycles, including road bikes, trail bikes, custom bikes, monkey bikes and quads in our new catalogue.

We had a steady stream of visitors from the Chinese plants, to look at the modifications we were doing on their bikes, to make them more suitable for the western markets, and we found the Chinese were very quick learners.

In India, Monto had made a new, two speed automatic Garelli engine and increased the capacity to 60cc, so they sent two sample engines to us for testing and we made a slightly bigger bike for this 60cc motor to fit in. This would now give us two Champ Garelli

Some of the Chinese bikes we did development work on

More Chinese bikes we did developement work on

engined bikes, a Champ SX50cc and a Champ SX60cc.

Next in line for development was a small quad, which again was to be built strong enough to carry a full sized adult. Mr Mehter invited John and Ellen to the factory to help them design and make the prototype. This was the first trip John and Ellen had ever made to India and when they arrived it was a bit of a culture shock for them. Dinesh Tandon, Mr Mehter's nephew, was at the Airport to meet them. He was assigned to work with us in developing the kids bike range for the European market. Dinesh took them to a local hotel and booked them in for their overnight stay but Ellen refused to enter the room when she saw six or seven Gecko's running up the walls. Dinesh was a bit taken aback as in India they are regarded as good luck, and besides that, they kept the flies down. Seeing Ellen was upset John insisted that he book them into another hotel. The second hotel was a much better class of accommodation as it only had one Gecko in the room. Both of them were, by this time, so tired that the lone Gecko was totally disregarded.

Dinesh was back at 7 o'clock the next morning with a car to take them to the Monto Motors moped factory at Alwar, a six hour drive away. John wasn't very impressed by the driver who, on two occasions, when the road was busy in front of him, switched across to the opposite side of the dual carriage way, driving into the oncoming traffic, at the same time telling John not to worry as he had done this for many years without having a crash. John said the look on Dinesh's face confirmed he thought the driver was mad too. After three hours Dinesh instructed the driver to pull over to what loosely could be described as a road side café. After a strong cup of coffee and some sort of burger they resumed their trip to the factory which was still another three hours away.

Eventually they arrived at the factory at about two in the afternoon where Mr Chand Mehter and Mr Talwar his deputy were waiting to greet them. They had just taken delivery of four brand new American CNC machines and had been waiting for their guests to arrive so they could take part in the blessing ceremony of these machines.

The entire plant stopped work to watch the ceremony which involved saying many prayers and giving the machines food offerings and draping garlands of flowers over them. John asked Dinesh what the ceremony was all about and was told it was to keep the new machines happy in their work.

Lunch had been arranged in the factory canteen for the visitors and according to John and Ellen the standard of food was very good, in fact he commented that the factory was absolutely immaculate inside, compared to the almost shanty town conditions outside, surrounding the factory. The factory was guarded by a large group of monkeys which patrolled the entire factory grounds, and became very threatening and alarming if anybody new appeared on the scene. When crossing the factory compound the monkeys took an instant dislike to John and Ellen so Mr Mehter ordered two of the Indian workforce, equipped with sticks, to sort the monkeys out and quieten them down. Jokingly Dinesh said.

'The monkeys must be colour prejudiced because of your white skin John.' Back in the factory's experimental workshop John was shown the prototype kids quad the Indians had made. He said to Mr Mehter.

'Realistically it looks like a couple of 5 year old kids have made it, no way do I want to sell that. The wheels and tyres are OK, the engines OK, but the rest needs to go in the scrap bin.' Their chief designer didn't look too pleased when John's comments were translated to him. John sat down with a piece of paper and did a quick sketch of an easy to make quad frame. For the market the quad was going into, it didn't need suspension front and rear, so the suspension on their prototype, which was too solid anyway, was discarded. John showed Dinesh some three quarter inch, 3 mm thick steel tubing which was lying on a workbench and asked if there was anymore lengths of this size in the factory.

'No but we can get some here by tomorrow morning.'

'OK if you can get more of this tubing we'll make a start on making a new chassis in the morning. How far away is the hotel because both me and Ellen are feeling quite tired now.'

'No problem, the hotel is only 5 minutes away and I will go with you, to make sure your accommodation is acceptable.' By the standards of the two previous hotels this one was very up market and after a good nights sleep and breakfast at eight o'clock they returned to the factory feeling refreshed. The tubing was already in the workshop when John arrived and Dinesh and the chief designer were both assigned to help John construct the new quad chassis. Their designer couldn't believe how John worked. John said he had the basis of the quad chassis cut to length and tacked up within an hour and it was taken to the welding shop to be fully welded, which took them about two hours.

When it came back John fitted the front and rear axles to it, the front steering pivots were cut on each side and leant back 15 degrees for better steering. Their steering pivots were literally upright, without any lean back angle. They had obviously never heard of the Ackerman Principle on steering angles. By dinner time the quad was sat on the floor on all four wheels. Then the handle bars were cut and lowered three inches, as they had been far too high. The fibre glass bodywork the Indians had made for the quad was cut up and redesigned by John to look more modern and up to date. Dinesh gave orders for the quad to be stripped off and fully welded, then painted, and said it had to be back in the workshop, all finished, no later than two o'clock.

Dinner was in the works canteen again where Dinesh asked John what he thought of India. John described it as very interesting, he told them he was very impressed with the factory and the high standard of upkeep there. Mr Mehter said that the factory was originally built for making refrigerators and freezers. It then switched over to making Lambretta scooters under licence from Italy, but they couldn't make them at a competitive enough price to sell in India, so they were only manufactured for two years before it closed. Monto had eventually bought the factory and done a deal with Garelli in Italy to make complete Garelli mopeds there and sell them in India. This was the time proven engine we were using in our kids bikes.

Although I was thousands of miles away I knew exactly what was happening every day. I remember when John and Ellen returned from India the phone bill for the period they were away was a total of £930 for the week.

Nev Mason
saying
1995
If you want to expand your empire you have no choice but to trade with the world

Prototype bikes we developed but never
produced because of the Mafia

Prototype bikes we developed but never
produced because of the Mafia

Chapter 19

Shortly after John's Indian visit I had a meeting with Fergal Sharkey at a big Record Company in London, now their department manager, he was looking for new talent. A great guy to get on with, he gave me many tips on how to avoid the pitfalls in the music industry. First tip; don't waste your time and money promoting your Russian groups here in the UK, this is a very corrupt business, you will get ripped off and it will cost you a fortune in bribes just to get air play for them. Second; I think you would be much better off promoting them in Russia and all the former Soviet bloc countries because, now they are signed to you at RTX Records in England, their credibility in their own country will be much higher. They must be good, that's why a western company has signed them up. Third; don't take on more groups than you can comfortably handle. Fourth; get plenty of video footage of the groups you like best, as stills are not much good for promoting them with.

Thanking him for his time and advice I returned home. Chris knew two guys in Grimsby who did video work so we went to see them to inquire if they had any interest in going to Russia to shoot some footage of the bands, all expenses paid, all they had to take was their video cameras. I would buy the tapes for the cameras and when they returned back home to the UK, all the completed tapes would belong to RTX Records. This they agreed to do and one week later we were getting off the plane in Lithuania, where Sash met us in a large bus he had procured from somewhere.

I had brought 100 copies of the new Krama CD, 'Vodka on Ice' with me, and Krama were on the bus with Sash eager to see and hear the first copy of their new Album, mixed and produced in England. I must admit by the time we got to Minsk I was sick and tired of hearing it as they continuously played it over and over again. If I use the word ecstatic that would be the correct definition, Krama were absolutely over the moon with the sound quality on the CD. The mixing had been done to the bands total satisfaction.

Arriving at Minsk, Krama disappeared into the distance still playing their new CD on their portable player. Sash had booked us into the Chess Palace, a large hotel type building where, apart from the rooms, chess tournaments were staged. It had been very grand at one time but was still very comfortable, though you could get bed and breakfast for $2 a night each. He had also booked, for the next day, the use of a variety hall in Minsk and had arranged for 14 of our top groups to be there at nine o'clock to video and record two tracks each. We managed to finish the session by eleven o'clock that night, and then moved on to the Mozyr recording studio the next day. Krama, Red Dynamite, Mirror Reflection, White Stream X and Paradox were all lined up over the next five days to do their video shoots and record some tracks, both in the studio and outside at a sports complex.

While they were doing this I nipped back to Minsk to the factory where Sev had just had the first mono disc, RTX MD 212 trials bike assembled. It looked well, and me and Sev spent most of the afternoon giving it a good work over on the off road track at the Minsk plant. After two hours we both had had enough and I told him to go ahead and make a batch of 20 and put them in the next container due for shipping to us. This done Sev booked tickets for us on the overnight train to Moscow, so we went to his apartment in Victory Square to have tea, which Irena had prepared for us, along with sandwiches to take with us on the train.

We caught the train at 11 pm that night in Minsk, and arrived in a freezing cold, ice covered Moscow at 6 am the next morning. Thankfully the kart factory's car was waiting for us, so we didn't have to hang around in the cold. Arriving at the factory we were taken to the canteen for breakfast and after a typical Russian early morning meal it was off to the directors office for negotiations on the warranty and prices etc., for the karts. It took us nearly all morning to sort everything out and in the end 500 complete karts were ordered, to be fitted with the standard Minsk engines for the first year, so we instantly became the biggest kart supplier in the UK overnight.

Next, we had an appointment at a very large tyre factory which made Moto Cross tyres, kart tyres, tyres for cars, trucks, aircraft, tractors and giant earthmovers. We were given a full tour of the factory and at about four pm a full board meeting had been set up to discuss the tyres. I counted 23 other people around the table. They brought in four sample tyres to show us. The tread patterns were quite modern and they looked well made. I noticed each tyre had a rubber inner tube fitted inside it, and asked if the price of each tyre included the inner tube. I was told that you just pay for the tyre and the tube comes free with it.

'So every tyre you sell has a free tube in it?' Sev asked, this was confirmed by the Director of the factory.

'Yes that is correct.' he said.

'Sev, please ask him how long they have been giving away free inner tubes with every tyre they make.' Everyone around the table just looked blankly at each other, it was just as I thought, this was something that nobody at the factory had ever asked before.

'When was this factory opened?' I asked.

'It started production in 1934, but why do you ask us this question Mr Mason?' the Director said to me.

'You have just given us a full tour of your plant, and I noticed that at least thirty percent of your factory is assigned to making inner tubes.

'Yes that figure is about correct.' With Sev translating I said.

'I find this all very interesting. Nearly one third of your factory is costing you, every week, money for wages, materials, running costs, and equipment to make these inner tubes, which you then give away, free of charge with each tyre you sell. This means you get no income at all from the inner tube manufacturing side of your plant. You are now a Private Ltd Company since Communism went?' I said to the Director.

'Yes that's correct, but what should we do? If we don't give our customers free tubes perhaps they may not buy our tyres.'

'I will personally guarantee you that they will still buy your tyres. Your customers need them, particularly in a developing market like Russia. Do you know any other factories in Russia that gives away its products free of charge?'

'No' the Director replied 'I don't.'

'The way to solve the problem is very easy, charge for every tube you make, don't just give them away, then the tube division will be able you make you a profit or at least earn enough money to cover its expenses.'

'Thank you very much Mr Mason for your positive advice to our company.' We agreed on a price of £1 per tyre in sizes 400 x 18 and 300 x 21, and 35 pence per kart tyre.

'And because you gave us such constructive advice Mr Mason, to you only, the tubes are free with all your tyres.' I gave him an order for 25000 MX tyres which were distributed for us in the UK by Cambrian Tyres, plus 20000 kart tyres. All the people around the table were thanked for coming to meet us and the Director personally gave us a lift back to the station in his car. Coming back to Minsk on the train Sev asked me why I gave them the advice on the tubes.

'Sev, I gave it because, in a free market, without the income from the inner tube side of the factory, they would eventually go bankrupt, and if they go bankrupt, I can't buy the tyres from them, and if I can't buy their tyres, I can't make a profit.'

'Ok Nev now I understand why you told them about the tubes. I'm very slowly beginning to see how your way of Western thinking is totally different from my Belarus way of thinking.'

The two video friends of Chris from Grimsby had managed to shoot plenty of video footage of the bands, both in Minsk and Mozyr, and on our return to England they spent five days editing and putting all the video shots into separate 4 minute showcases, one for each band, and then the top 12 groups were put onto a 48 minute long master tape which was entitled 'So You Think The Russians Can't Play Rock and Roll'. This tape proved that they could rock with the best.

I now had a guy working for me full time in Belarus promoting the bands. Fergal Sharkey had been right. The bands had increased interest in them, both in Russia and all the former communist countries now they were signed up to a western company, just as he had predicted.

Sev rang me a week after I got back and said the Motovelo factory at Minsk had a very big problem. Now that Yeltsin had declared that Communism was dead and gone in Russia forever, and since his take over from the Gorbachev regime, all the former USSR countries had declared their independence of Russia. Belarus stated it was free of Moscow and it was now the Sovereign State of Belarus. They had even designed a new national flag for the new state, which, incidentally changed two weeks later to another new design, but that's another story.

Avtoexport in Moscow, it seems, had looked after the money from sales for Motovelo for the last 16 years, because they paid a better rate of interest than the banks did. The money owed to Motovelo, I was told, amounted to $420960 and Avtoexport told them that because Belarus was now a separate and independent state all the money now belonged to

Russia, and they could not have it. This put the Minsk Factory in a very bad position financially. Sev explained to me that unless they received positive Government help they could go Bankrupt. The Government must have helped them because suddenly the crisis was over and everything seemed to return to normal.

Me and Val visited the factory five weeks later to sort out the new reduced prices and this was to be a trip I would always remember. We stayed at the Chess Palace again as it was a very tidy place and good value for money. A visit to see Dr Albert Lavrenov at the hospital was organized by Sev, and we were shocked to find Albert was carrying a gun in his pocket, as protection he said, against the new Mafia who were now operating in the hospital complex. They were trying to force all the staff to give them 15% of their individual weekly wages. This had all happened, Albert explained, since Communism was abolished. Even so, it was nice to meet John's former doctor again and we spent a pleasant afternoon with him, drinking and reminiscing.

Shortly after this meeting Albert and all his family were helped to move to the USA, with some organised assistance from a very grateful friend. Who it was I cannot say.

What was now about to take place, at several meetings Sash had organised at the Chess Palace for the next few day, spies would have died for in the not so distant past. Many of the 'Top Secret' Russian State inventions I was about to be offered, were quite mind blowing. The meetings Sash had organised for me and Val were with, what I can only really describe as 'mad scientists'. The fall of Communism had meant that each Director, of their particular institute, or college, had sort of inherited all the business they had been working on, becoming the owner of whatever project they were involved with.

**A VERY DRUNKEN JOURNALIST AT
EARLS COURT SHOW, AFTER BEING GIVEN
ACCESS TO OUR RUSSIAN VODKA SAID,
'NEV YOU CAN BE A BASTARD, BUT AT LEAST
YOU ARE A GENUINE BASTARD.'
HE ADDED THAT THIS WAS MEANT AS A
COMPLIMENT TO ME.
QUOTE FROM A WELL KNOW M/C JOURNALIST**

Chapter 20

That evening we went to Sev's apartment for a special Belorussian version of Hot Pot with him, Irena and his kids. We had a very pleasant, family oriented time before returning to the Chess Palace and bed. The following morning we had breakfast with Sash, and when this was finished we followed him down a long length of corridor at the rear of the Chess Palace where he had arranged for a room to be made available for us to have preliminary business talks with the various research scientists who had approached him for advice on cooperation with England, with their previously state sponsored projects. It was well known in Minsk that Sash worked for an English businessman. This was to be the most interesting three days I ever spent in Belarus.

The first meeting was with a scientist who had been working on his project for eleven years. Without getting too technical, his project involved finding a cure for radiation sickness. What his institute had come up with was a tablet that had to be taken, a minimum of one hour before exposure to radiation. This pill, when taken, we were told, coated the blood cells and stopped them absorbing the radiation. He produced a bottle of brown aspirin sized tablets and put them on the table for examination. Sash, through translation, explained to us that 116 academics had worked on this project and that the tablets were made using pine needles as the base ingredient. We were asked if we were interested in buying these tablets to sell. I explained that this was not my area, so was not interested in buying them personally, but if he gave Sash his contact details, when I returned to the UK I would contact Chemical companies to try and find one that would work directly with them.

The second scientist was then invited in by Sash. His project involved cattle food. He had worked on this program for seven years and had developed and built a special machine at his university which, if you put half a ton of normal cattle food in at one end, one ton in weight came out of the other end. They had devised some system to bulk up and double the weight of the food as it passed through the machine. Again this was not my area so I said I would try to source a partner in the UK for him.

The third of Sash's scientists arrived and I asked Sash what his university had developed, looking embarrassed he said

'It's a gun, Nev, but a special gun.'

'Sash, I do not deal in guns or have anything to do with guns.'

'Just let the guy explain to you what it is. Basically he says it's a death ray gun and he's says he has worked on this project for eighteen years along with 180 of his colleagues. It's already here, he has a sample downstairs if you want to have a look at it.' Curiosity got the better of me so I followed Sash and Igor the scientist, down the stairs and out into the rear car park, where there was a four by four Uaz pickup in army camouflage colours, with what looked to me, like a large generator mounted at the cab end of the body, and the gun itself mounted on a swivel with a seat behind it, and about a six foot long barrel, which was approximately nine inches in diameter. Igor asked Sash if I wanted a demonstration of the guns powers, explaining they could take it out into the countryside and demonstrate it on a cow if I wanted them to.

'No thanks I have seen enough.' The three of us returned to the room where more explanations were given about the possible uses.

I asked Igor what had been the guns original use

before they had developed it into a weapon and he explained that eighteen years before, the original use had been a machine to scan the brain for tumours, but some bright spark had found out that if the power was raised by a certain amount the brain heated up and literally melted inside the scull.

They developed this weapon which, he said, originally had a range of two metres, but, he claimed, it now had a range of just over one kilometre, and what I described as a gun on the back of the pickup, was in actual fact a device to funnel the beam into a concentrated area. If it was fired at a tank he said it would kill the crew but leave the tank intact. They had now also developed it so it could be fired from a plane.

My personal thoughts were, that this is serious stuff. I told Igor that if you make this weapon public knowledge there's a good chance that the wrong people could get hold of it and it could be used against you and your country in the future. The best thing you could do is dismantle what working samples you have and I will try to get someone interested in the west to use the technology for its original use of brain scanning.

It was now time for lunch and me, Val and Sash

went to the Planeta Hotel where Albert joined us. I asked Sash if there were any more people to see that day as the novelty was starting to wear off. He told me there were two more meetings arranged for the afternoon, so after lunch we returned to the Chess Palace to continue the meetings with Sash's contacts.

'What's next' I asked him as in marched a very large gentleman carrying a fair sized wooden box which he put on the table in front of himself. Sash talked to him for a few minutes.

'He says it's a totally new type of motorcycle engine he and his colleagues at the college have developed over the last seven years.' Now it became like a cartoon set.

'Can I see the engine, I presume its in the box Sash?'

'No Nev, he says you can't see it, he's frightened to let you see the engine in case you describe it to any other people.'

'So he wants me to try and sell the idea of this new engine to any interested parties in the UK without them seeing it. Tell him to go away and think about it, how does he expects anybody to have an interest in the engine if they can't see it, tell him thanks for coming and good bye.'

'Ok lets have the last one in for today then Sash.' Dear me I thought, this guy looks like the original Dick Dastardly.

'What's he selling?' I asked Sash. This did not look good as yet again he looked very embarrassed.

'He says he has some Red Mercury balls to sell.'

'What the hell are they?' I asked him.

'I think they are to make a bomb Nev.'

'What have you brought him in here for? Why would I want to make a bloody bomb?'

'But Nev, these are worth a lot of money and he has five of them in a box in the boot of his Lada car outside, he only wants $50 each for them.'

'Sorry Sash but tell him I am not interested in them.' Dick Dastardly went out of the door looking a bit put out. I often wondered who bought them from him.

We were just leaving as the engine guy reappeared at the door with a pile of papers in his hands.

'Nev, he says if you sign all these papers he will let you see the engine.'

'What are the papers for Sash?'

'To say that you will not show pictures of this engine to anybody without asking his permission.' I signed the five papers and asked him to take the lid of the box. He unscrewed the lid and proudly lifted the engine out, putting it on the table. I took one look at it and said to Sash.

'What's supposed to be so special about this engine? How long have they been working on it, seven years?' Sensing something was wrong the director asked Sash if there was a problem.

'The problem is.' I said 'It would appear you and your colleagues have been working on this engine for the last seven years for no reason, I'm sorry, but this new design of engine, as you call it, was used in the west in the 1920 s. If I recollect right it had a UK patent granted and the design was used by the English firm Barr and Stroud, for their motorcycle engines, which had an internal, rotating port sleeve valve, inside the cylinder head, just as your engine seems to have. I know it was used by Alldays and Onions in their motorcycles in England but the performance was never as good as in conventional engines, and the design was eventually dropped. I find it fascinating that you didn't know that this design had been used and superseded in the west. His answer was a very sad, disappointed.

'Nobody told us this type of engine had been designed before. Thank you very much for telling me. My colleagues will also be very disappointed to hear this very bad news.'

Sash invited me and Val to his apartment for tea, and it would be the first time I had been to his home.

'I must be paying him to much.' I thought as I looked around his flat which was full of expensive western goods and audio equipment. His wife Nico had spent a lot of time and effort on a lavish meal for us. Sash said he hoped tomorrow was going to be a better day. He then asked if I was interested in off road buggies as a firm in Mogilev, who manufactured them, had contacted him. All Sash knew was that they were fitted with Minsk engines.

'Find out what you can about them.' I told him 'and try and get some photos so I can see what they look like, and then try and get a price on them.' After a very pleasant evening he ordered a taxi to take us back to the Chess Palace.

'See you in the morning Sash at 9.30 and don't be late. How many are we seeing tomorrow?'

'Four I think.' he said. At 9.35am, with no sign

of Sash or anybody else, we went down to the meeting room. The door was open so we went inside to wait and after about 20 minutes Sash finally arrived. His car had had a puncture and he didn't have a spare wheel with him so he'd had to walk.

A knock on the door announced the arrival of the next Director who spoke very good English.

'Hello, I am Alex my company makes and sells a new type of alloy radiator. It's a radical new method of production which our college has developed over the last 11 years.' In explanation he told us.

'We take a block of high grade aluminium and cut grooves in it to form the cooling fins on the outside, then a router cuts down the middle of the block so the cooling liquid can pass through it. We can make all types and sizes of alloy cooling radiators from trucks to motorcycles.' He showed us photos of some sample radiators and they looked a real quality piece of kit.

'Alex, if I was to send you a pair of Honda MX radiators could you copy them using your manufacturing method?'

'Yes I could.' he answered. Then I remembered Motovelo had two CR Honda MX bikes which they sponsored Volodya Esiavich on, so I rang Sev and asked if he could borrow a pair of radiators off one of the bikes and bring them over. He arrived in the room with a pair of Honda rads 50 minutes later and Alex took them, promising to return the originals to Sev and send a sample set by airfreight to us in England within a week. He also left with me photos and a full list of car and truck radiators they could already manufacture at his college, and asked if I could try to find customers in the UK for them. This could be a good business opportunity. We thanked him for coming to see us. Sev as a designer, was really interested in the unique way they were made.

Sash brought in the next guy who had been waiting outside for an hour.

'I am Mikhail Kling.' and my company is involved with a special Government dept in Belarus selling fertilizer. It is good quality, and we can supply up to a maximum of 2500 tons of fertilizer a week, and because it is a good stuff we want £20 a ton for it.' I told him it was not of interest to me, but there may be people in the UK who would be interested in buying it and said I would check on my return to England. He left all his contact details with us and went. Sash said that he had heard the fertilizer they were selling was dirty or contaminated and that's why it was so cheap.

'So why did you invite him here then Sash?

'I thought you could probably get it cleaned up.' was his answer. Words failed me.

The next guy waiting outside was invited in. His name was Anatoly and he was a Director at an Aircraft Development Factory located in the Ukraine. He put on the table a piece of alloy about 6x6 inches square and it was so thin and light, if you blew on it would have blown away.

'This alloy is the thickness of a human hair.' he said 'please try bending it.' I did and could not believe just how strong it was.

'We have spent many, many years developing this alloy to be used to cover aircraft wings and body parts. It makes these parts very light and strong, plus it makes the aircraft also very fast in operation. My factory is very interested in working with a western aircraft company in a joint cooperation with them.'

'Can I take the alloy sample with me when I return to England.' I asked.

'Yes of course you can, but please look after it and don't lose it.'

'I will take good care of it for you. There is a big aircraft factory near my home in England, I will approach them when I return to the UK, to see if they have any interest in a joint cooperation with your plant.' Sash thanked him for coming to see me.

The next guy in was called Boris Ferdman.

'We have this to sell.' He put on the table three pieces of what looked to be wood, but were very heavy and felt like marble to the touch.

'This material can be cut or drilled or have a thread tapped into it. It's as hard as metal and can be used to make almost anything, that can normally be made from wood. It has many uses for manufacturing items for the market place.'

'Is this granite.' I asked him, 'or some other form of rock?' he smiled and shook his head.

'No, it started life as a pine tree, which we put inside a ceramic chamber, then treat it with special rays to alter its molecular structure, changing it from soft wood to hard wood.'

'And what sort of rays do you use on it?' Sash asked him.

'We use Radiation to change its structure.'

'Radiation, did he just say what I thought he

said?' I asked Sash.

'Yes Nev, you heard him correctly.' replied Sash, backing away from the table. Me and Val now joined him at the other end of the room.

'Sash' I said 'Please tell him to take the samples with him when he goes, we will let him know if there is any interest in his products in England.' Never ever have I been so glad to see anybody leave. We all waved him good buy and quickly shut the door.

It was lunch time so we had a meal in the Chess Palace for a change, and over dinner we discussed Ferdman's offer of his version of hard wood. All were in agreement to forget it. How could you sell anything that had been subjected to radiation in its manufacture. Then there was the matter of the Red Mercury balls and also the dirty, contaminated fertilizer. I gave Sash a right ear bashing and told him not to waste my time with this type of stupid project in the future, by the time I had finished I think he had got the message but there were still two more people to see today after we finished eating.

Albert had arrived during lunch to take Val to the shops to buy a watch she wanted. It was a Seconda which would cost about £60 plus in England but in

Belarus it was only a few roubles, the equivalent of about £3 in sterling.

Waiting outside the room on our return was a guy who wanted to sell me some Belarus tractors which were made in Minsk. The fact that they were already imported into England did not seem to bother him or Sash at all. I had no interest in them but they insisted that I go and look around the factory which was only just down the road. The massive size of the plant was quite impressive and it had two very long production lines, side by side. One had red tractors being assembled on it and was a hive of activity with all the parts being tested and the engines being started up. The tractors were then run on a rolling road before being dispatched to a special department for further checking before going for export. The other line had blue tractors on it and I was told these were for the Russian internal market. Sash asked me,

'Do you want to buy any of the red export tractors? They can give you a good discount if you order five hundred tractors a month from them.'

'Sash, I came here because you and your mate invited me but I told you before I came that I am not interested in dealing in tractors thanks.'

Chapter 21

Back in the room, the next director arrived. Vasily was from the off road buggy factory at Mogilev that had contacted Sash previously. This was more like it, I got quite excited when he produced photos of the buggies. They had a full roll cage type chassis, independent suspension, front and rear disc brakes and 700 x 10 balloon off road tyres. They made two models, one with a standard Minsk 125cc engine and one with a Planeta 350cc engine. Both were full sized buggies and they had been in production for about nine years. The only problem I could see was that the paint used on the chassis was typically Russian, a miserable brown colour. When I asked why they used this dull, uninteresting colour I was told that the paint was only to protect the metal from rusting, and whatever colour the customer wanted would be put on, over the brown undercoat. There were four colours to choose from, red, yellow, blue and green. I asked what their best price for these buggies was and was told £120 each F.O.B. St Petersburg. I jokingly told him £100 would be better, to which he replied 'OK.'

I made arrangements for them to ship two

sample models to the UK for evaluation. One of each model, with one in red and one in blue. He then explained that the buggy section was only a very small division of their factory and the major production was making massive, 80 ton, articulated Earth Movers, with 10 litre, V8 diesel engines fitted at the front and rear, and also huge, 70 ton, Dump Trucks fitted with V10 diesel engines. Now that Avtoexport no longer sold the trucks and scrapers for them, they needed new contacts and asked if I would be interested in buying them, or in finding a new contact for them, as they were geared up only to manufacturing and had no selling department of their own. I asked them what major countries they had previously sold them to, and found his reply quite mind blowing.

'I don't know, they never told us who the buyers were, or even what countries they went to, because they also arranged all the shipping and deliveries.' I asked him how many he had in stock and if they were still being produced, and was told they had 316 in stock.

The problem was the various factories that supplied them with components for future production. They were all still working, producing the parts, because if they stopped, the workers would have

Top: Buggies we designed with Honda engines
Bottom: Road scraper made in Minsk

Some of the steam trains I found in Byelorussia

nothing to do. These factories relied on the factory and had no other outlets. They had no income at all since Belarus had declared itself independent of Moscow, months previously. They had the same situation that Motovelo had. Previously, Aftoexport had looked after, and kept all their money, and had now told them to clear off, they couldn't have their money back as they were now a separate state.

'So how are you paying your workers?' I asked him.

'We have no money to pay them with, or any to pay our suppliers.'

'So your workers are still coming to work in the factory, even though they are not being paid?'

'Yes, I have told them we will pay them when we have some money, what else can I do? If you can visit our factory you will see the machines we produce and we can demonstrate them working for you.' I made arrangements to go to the factory on my next visit to Belarus, as it was only a 2 hour drive away from Minsk. Shaking hands with him I told him I would see him then. As he departed he said he would also arrange demonstrations of his dump trucks for us .

The next guy entered in full battle dress and sat

down at the table. He explained that his battalion, now that Belarus was an independent state, had too many tanks and was I interested in buying any, or did I know anybody who might be interested in them. He had 100 fully serviced T34 tanks to sell. I looked across at Sash.

'Did you know what this guy was selling Sash, before he came in?' I asked.

'Yes, but I thought they were very cheap, he only wants $1000 each for them.'

'Are they all still fully armed and still capable of operating?'

'Yes, he says they are.'

'The only market I can see for them Sash, is if the guns can be permanently disarmed, and any war orientated equipment stripped out of them, then they could probably sell them in the off road market for leisure use, letting people pay to drive them off road. I know a guy in England who does this sort of thing so I will ring him when I get back, but I never did ring him.'

'He also has 5000 AK47 machine guns.' Sash said. He knew by the look I gave him he was treading on shaky ground yet again. Jokingly I said.

'Tell him if he rings Yeltsin up in Moscow he'll

probably buy them.'

'Is that everybody you've arranged for me to see then Sash?' I asked.

'No, Nev there is one more proposition left for you.'

'I hope its quick I want to go to the Planeta after this for a rest and a drink. OK Sash, who is it?'

'It's a guy who is in charge of running the railway system in all of Belarus, he's the director and controls everything, he says he has 116 old steam trains parked up at Osopovichy, some are in good running condition and others require some work on them, but he wants to know if you can find him any customers, steam train enthusiasts, who would want to come and ride in them, and look at them for a holiday, as he says he has been told that these type of train trips are very popular in England.'

'Ask him if it is possible for us to look at them.'

'Yes, he says we can go tomorrow if you want to.' So the next morning we were on a train to Osopovichy to have a look at them. I had no real interest in trains apart from finding any old machinery like this very interesting. When we arrived it was indeed quite amazing just how many old steam trains there were, parked up in the sidings. They had two absolutely massive trains that he told us were the biggest ever built in Russia. One of them was puffing steam out of its boiler, and they had it plugged into some nearby greenhouses where they were cultivating tomatoes. I spent about an hour taking photos of many of them, then we were invited to lunch at the local restaurant where the Director explained he also had many old carriages for the trains to pull. After a long lunch we returned back to Minsk and Sash said he would get the guy to work out some provisional prices for five day trips with the restaurant car and the sleeping carriages included in the price.

As we were leaving the Chess Palace Albert and Val arrived back from visiting Irena. It was mid afternoon and as we went through the Planeta front doors Sash was stopped by a group of three, well dressed men who talked with him for about five minutes. Albert was due back on duty so left to go to the hospital and over our drinks I asked Sash who the three men he had been talking to were, and he told me they were Government men.

'The middle guy was the Deputy Prime Minister of Belarus, the tall guy at the end is the

Minister for Business and Education and the third guy, I don't know.' he said 'but by the bulge in his pocket I would say he was their protector. They asked if it was possible to have a meeting with you later today.'

'What do they want a meeting with me about?' I asked puzzled.

'They want to ask your advice on certain things, as you are the only English person who is well known in Belarus, and they know you have dealt here, with Motovelo, for over 20 years.' The tall guy was still waiting by the door so I told Sash to tell him it was no problem we would go. We finished our drinks and feeling a bit more refreshed we asked Sash to order a taxi.

'No need.' he said. 'They are sending a car for you, to take you to the Parliament buildings where their office is situated.' A few minutes later a Government car pulled up outside the Hotel and we were whisked off in great style, in a large black limousine. On arrival we were escorted down a very long, red carpeted, corridor where the Ministers were waiting to receive us. They both spoke only a bit of English so Sash was asked to translate.

'Mr and Mrs Mason, thank you for coming, we

would like to ask your advice on certain matters concerning the running of our new Independent State of Belarus.' This cannot be true I thought, me and Val, sitting here at a conference table in the Ministers office, and they want advice from me on how to run their country. A secretary then came in to take notes.

'Mr Mason do you think it is a good idea for us to issue visas for entry to Belarus or would it be best to have an open border with no visas issued?'

'If you don't have entry visas how do you know who is coming in or going out of your country?' I asked him. 'I really don't see how you can operate all your many border crossings without using visas.'

'Thank you for that advice. How do you think we can get Western Business Partners to invest in Belarus with us?'

'That's a very simple question,' I said, 'just offer them a good deal, with security for all their investments, coupled with low tax incentives for the first few years. That will almost guarantee you will get their interest.'

'Would you invest here Mr Mason?

'I have been investing in Belarus, through Motovelo, for the last 20 years.' I replied. 'and plus, I now have 24 of the best Rock Bands in Belarus signed to me through my English company RTX Records UK.'

'We do know about your many years helping Motovelo but we didn't know about your RTX Record company. Are all your groups from our country?'

'Yes they are.' I said

'And are they any good compared to Western bands?' he asked me.

'Yes most are as good as any bands I have heard in the west.' He obviously liked rock music.

'Have you heard of Krama?' he asked me 'They are very good.'

'Yes I know they are good, they were the first group I signed to RTX Records. Their first CD album titled Vodka on Ice is soon to be released.'

'When are you back in Belarus Mr Mason?'

'In about four weeks.' I said to them.

'Would you be interested in conducting a business class for us?'

'What exactly do you mean?' I asked.

'Many of our business people have no idea how western business works, they only know how communist business works. We need someone from the west like you, with years of experience to teach them basic business etiquette, and what the best way of working with western business partners is. We would pay you for this two day seminar.'

'You don't have to pay me, I'm not motivated by money, just make sure I have somewhere decent to sleep and some good food, that will be enough.' It was suggested that Berezinski Park would be the ideal place as it had modern buildings and teaching facilities. It was a wild life reserve with full conference facilities. The same car that brought us to the meeting now took us back to the Chess Palace and just as Sash was leaving Sev arrived. He said I had to ring John urgently. After waiting about an hour to get a line to England I was finally put through to John.

'Sorry but its bad news Dad, your Mother died in Hospital late last night.' What do you say at a time like this, suddenly all the feelings I had when my Dad and Burt had died came flooding back, all I could think of to say to John was,

'We will try to get a train back tomorrow.' then I rang off. It's not often I have cried as an adult but with tears flooding down my face, I told Val the news, then we were both in tears.

Sev managed to book a earlier train for us to

return to England. My brother Pete was very upset with me because I had not been there when Mam had died, but I learned many years ago that you can't be in two places at once. We buried Mam at her birthplace, Skidby near Hull, and the funeral was a very sad occasion for all the family. At times like this you reflect on just how short life really is.

A week after the funeral Sash sent a fax regarding the steam trains. It seems the proposed steam train trips could travel anywhere in Belarus, and could even use the old military train lines, which were previously banned from public use. If I could get any interest in England for these unique excursions the price was to be $150 per person, per trip, for the five days, which seemed a reasonable price to me. A travel agent in Hull was very interested in being the agent and organising these trips, but being Belarus, because I had now got some interest in the trips, the price went up to $200 each by the end of the week. They claimed a mistake in the costing had been made on the first price. Another week passed while I sat waiting for the next inevitable price increase to arrive and sure enough on the Monday morning it came.

'Sorry Nev but again their calculations were out,

the price has to be $300 per person.' I faxed back to Sash to say sorry but the price is now too expensive, so forget the steam train trips, and within one hour back came his reply.

'Ok, he now says they can do the trips for $250.'

'Sorry Sash but I'm no longer interested in his proposition, tell him to get stuffed. Without stability in the prices it's a non starter.' A week passed by when up popped another fax from Sash.

'Nev they say the price is now down to $195 per person.'

'Sash, I'm sorry, but these people are not stable to work with. I have no further interest in this project at all, so just forget it.'

Nev Mason
saying
2000
You cannot do everything yourself, learning to delegate to others is the key to success.

Chapter 22

A long month had gone by, and me and Pete Ralph were on our way back to Belarus to record some of the other bands at the Mozyr Studios, then we were to carry on and visit Motovelo to check if all the modifications we had asked for had been done on the next batch of RTX Trials bikes, and to see if Sash's mates still wanted me to do the business seminar. Sash met us on our arrival and took us straight to the Parliament Buildings where the Ministers were waiting for us. We were ushered into a large conference room where lots of smart, suited, business people were gathered around a massive table.

'What's all this about?' I asked Sash.

'Nev, they are proposing to you, a business tie up between Belarus and England and they want to call it BELANG.' As we walked in they had just finished taking a vote and Mr Neville Mason had been elected as the Co President, representing the English side of the board. The elected President of the Belarus side of the board was Mr Leonid Sechko, while the secretary was Valery Serdyuk. The Business Minister asked me if I was OK with all this, then went on to ask if it was possible to have the first day of the business seminar the next day at Berizinsky Park. I couldn't see any reason why not, so we made the arrangements and left the Parliament Buildings to go to Motovelo, but on arrival, were shocked to find it closed.

Sash telephoned Sev to find out why, and Sev explained that the factory's director, Constantine Ustymchuck's 16 year old son had been stabbed and killed earlier in the day by a new Mafia gang in Minsk, that was trying to take over inside the Motovelo factory. The workers had all walked out in sympathy and shut the plant down. Sev also said that both the Bear and the Weasel had not been seen since the previous day and it was feared they also had been forcibly removed by this new Mafia, as two people reported that they had seen them being pushed into the back of a van and then driven off.

All this was a bit too much for me and Pete so I suggested to Sash that we go to the Chess Club and book into our rooms. After spending a very restless night at the club we were collected after breakfast and taken to Berezinsky Park for the business meeting. I counted 37 future, potential business tycoons around the huge conference table. The chairman had a list of

Presidential Building, Minsk, where I was voted in
as Chairman of Belang

The Chess Palace at Minsk

32 questions he had brought with him, and many of these just required a simple yes or no answer.

I told them that the major thing they must learn in dealing with Western business men, is the ability to create trust with them, because if they feel they cannot trust you they will refuse to work with your companies. You just have to be truthful and honest with them.

I suggested they consider a plan to organize a big exhibition in London showing all the products that they manufacture here in Belarus and all the services they can offer to England, and they did organize an exhibition at Earls Court in London about six months later which was very successful for Belarus.

With the seminar now over I borrowed from a park ranger a standard 125 Minsk, which had been built for the Russian market and bore no comparison to the Regent Minsk we had developed for our English market. After about 10 km I realised just how big this reserve was. There were no sign posts around just paths and tracks going in different directions.

In the distance I spotted what looked like a large herd of cows but as I got closer it suddenly dawned on me that these were not cows, they were bison, and very annoyed, bloody big, bison at that. They didn't seem to appreciate the sound of the Minsk 125 two stroke engine ringing around their woods and were starting to get very agitated.

Bombing off in the opposite direction, I hoped the bike would not run out of petrol, and after about 2 km I stopped and checked to see if the bison had followed me, but they hadn't thankfully. Getting lost in 1890 acres of forest may seem like heaven, but as panic began to set in, it became a fact that I was indeed well and truly lost. Wasn't this the place, they had told me yesterday, that still had black bears and genuine wild wolf packs wandering about in it? I checked the petrol tank which was luckily half full.

In the distance I heard another motorcycle engine and when the bike and rider came into view, I saw it was a park ranger on another 125 Minsk. I waved and he rode across to me, only it wasn't a he, it was a she. A girl of about 25 pulled up and in quite good English explained that the Park Director had sent three riders out to look for me as I had been gone for about 3 hours. I followed her back through the winding forest roads to the Directors house. Her name was Natasha, and she was his daughter.

Everybody seemed to think it was very funny, my having to be escorted back out of the woods by a young girl on a motorbike, but I must admit that 20 minutes earlier it hadn't looked like I was going to find my way back at all. I thanked Natasha for leading me back then Sash said that the Director's wife was preparing a special Belarusian celebration meal of boiled Carp for us.

After a quick wash and brush up, we all sat around the family table. The inevitable vodka was put on the table and we had to drink a toast to Belarus, followed by more toasts to all the people present, then the meal of the day was produced in a very large bowl.

It was filled to the top with what looked to me like slimy green Swarfega hand cleaner, with greenish, boiled carp heads sticking out of it. All the fish were complete with their eyes and fins and they all had their mouths gaping open.

'As we are the guests' Sash announced, 'we get all the best bits.'

'Oh, which are the best bits?' Pete asked him.

'The heads of course.' he was told, 'they are, what's that you say in English Nev, yum, yum.' Spooning a large portion onto his plate Sash salivated over the dish, with streaks of the green boiled slime running down his beard. The directors wife Neala, put some on mine and Pete's plates. Never in my life have I had such a compulsion to vacate a table. Me and Pete looked at each other, I think our thoughts were the same, do we really have to eat this stuff. Picking up a spoon I tried some.

'What does it taste like Nev?' Pete enquired hopefully.

'Well I think probably liquid gangrene is the best way to describe it.' I answered. The large fish bowl was now empty so was Sashs' plate so quick as a flash I asked him if he wanted any more.

'Yes I would like some but it's gone now.' he said pointed to the empty bowl.

'As a special treat to you Sash, you can have all mine.' Before he could change his mind I put my plate down in front of him and he tucked in with gusto. Boy was I glad to unload that lot. Pete looked on hoping Sash would finish mine and accept his plate as well but he had no such luck, Sash said that he had enjoyed the extra plate full, but he had now had enough and was full.

We talked for many hours about what future the

park had, now communism had gone, and how the park could support itself financially. I asked the Director how he thought it could generate income and he said he had already had people from Germany and Czechoslovakia contact him who wanted to come to Berezinski park to shoot the wildlife and he had had a phone call from someone in Canada who wanted to buy all the beavers in the park and come across to trap them for their fur.

I told him this would be an absolutely stupid decision to make. If he were to let this type of person into the park they would kill everything in sight. This park is the only one in Europe that has bison, wolves, wild boar, deer, black bears and beavers still living in the wild. The best way to give it a stable future is to make it a tourist attraction. There are many thousands of people in Europe who would travel here to see these animals in their natural habitat. If you allow the hunters in to kill them, they are gone forever, but if you allow tourists to come and see them, the park will have a guaranteed future and income for years to come, as you have something here to promote, that no-one else in Europe has.

We went to Mozyr recording studios from here

to collect some new tapes that Paradox and White Stream X had made, and to record some new Krama songs, then it was back to Minsk. I felt very ill by the time we arrived back at the Planeta hotel. A doctor was called by Sash to my room and within minutes he rang for an ambulance and I was taken to the local hospital, then, within one hour, I was transferred to the Minsk Parliament Hospital.

It seems I had picked up a chest infection which was causing me to have breathing problems. After many tests, and now stuffed full of antibiotics, I started to make a slow recovery. A doctor was sent from England to escort me back home on the plane. I was taken to Minsk Airport in a wheelchair with the escorting doctor and Pete, and as much as I hate travelling on planes, especially Russian ones, this particular time I didn't care, I felt too ill and just wanted to get home. The good part is it only took two hours for the plane to reach Manchester Airport, unlike travelling back by train which would have taken us two days.

On reaching Manchester there was an ambulance waiting for us and it took only another two hours to reach home, where everybody was waiting to greet me. It was good to be back and a week later I was able to get about without using the wheelchair. It was disappointing that I had not had the chance to visit the dump truck factory on this trip.

The first shipment of 50 of the new RTX 212 cc twin shock trials bikes arrived and they went out very quickly, as they were all, already pre ordered by dealers and customers. We kept two back from this shipment to use as demo bikes and that weekend me, John and Wayne gave both bikes a good work out around the local quarry at South Ferriby.

On the Monday morning, I was pleased to see that the first samples of the CR Honda radiators had arrived. They really looked great, and were lighter than the stock rads. John fitted them to a Honda CR 125 in the shop which was then taken out to our test track at the back of the shop and hammered around by John and Wayne for about two hours. They definitely ran cooler than the original rads and fitted straight onto the bike without any modifications being needed. In the afternoon John and Wayne took the bike to Ferriby quarry and ran it around for the afternoon without any problems.

The next day, I rang Alex in Minsk and told him

we had tested the sample rads he had sent us on a bike, and were happy with them, so could he prepare a batch of 250 matching pairs of CR125 Honda rads, 250 matching pairs of CR250 Honda Rads, and 250 matching pairs of CR500 Honda rads. I asked him how long will it would take to make and deliver them to us. I was told the 125 rads would be no problem but he would need sample 250cc and 500cc rads to copy. I arranged to send him these radiators by courier and he rang me when he had received the DHL shipment. He estimated that a total of two months would be needed to complete the order for all the radiators, plus one week to ship the completed order to us. I told him that would be ok, could he please make a start on the order and I would send him a cheque.

John took the sample pair of rads off the stock bike and took them to show Neal Tuxworth at Honda UK at Louth. Neal was very intrigued with the way they were made and offered to test them on one of their bikes. A week later he rang John and said he was amazed by the results of the tests. He said that on the test bed they ran 16 percent cooler than the standard Honda radiators and they weighed nearly one pound lighter, but Honda was not interested in using them as they were made in Russia.

Honda, it seems, didn't want to admit that the Russians could make something better than they could, but personally he was very impressed, especially when he was told that the same firm in Russia that made the sample CR125 Honda radiators he had tested were now making radiators, using the new method of construction they had invented, for Scania, MAN and Volvo Trucks. When the first production of Honda pattern radiators arrived from Alex we had a waiting list for them, and over the next 4 years we sold thousands of them worldwide.

Around this time I created a new type of small fun bike built for adults and kids using our Monto Garelli engined 50cc kids bike as a base to start from. It was fully stripped off until just the frame, wheels and engine remained and was fitted with a BMX type seat. In the three years it was in production we sold many thousands of these little fun bikes under our brand name TRAKA.

We made two models, the T 1 model which had no suspension front or rear, and no front brake, while the T 2 model had front and rear suspension and a disc front brake. What I did find very interesting was that the T I model always out sold the T 2 model.

Nev Mason
saying
1999
*Before you waste time and money inventing
something make sure there's a market for it.*

LESSONS IN LIFE

Don't rely on your friends to advise you in making
your business decisions they really don't want you to
do better in business than them, so make your own
decisions as you go through life, then if you are
wrong it's your fault, not theirs.

Leaflet for the new Traka I designed

John and his daughter Jade testing prototype Traka
on our airfield

Chapter 23

A major problem we now started to encounter at the Motovelo plant in Minsk was with the new Mafia in the factory. They were starting to cause trouble in our RTX department, first, by demanding from our workers, ten percent of their wages, then they told Sev, who ran the department, that they wanted $50 in cash for each bike that was produced, and $75 in cash for any new models we started to make in the future at the factory. Over the last year we had developed three new models for production in 1998, a new Enduro bike, a new Funcross bike, and a new Sports road bike.

These three bikes were ready to be put into production, but now, with the Mafia trying to impose their demands on us, I put an immediate hold on the new RTX projects. There was no way I was giving these bandits $50 or $75 a bike so it was back to Belarus for me yet again.

Sev met me at three in the morning at Minsk Railway Station and we went to his home to discuss the factory Mafia situation. He told me the workers had agreed to pay the mob $5 a week each out of their wages, and this seemed to me to be a small price to pay them, for a peaceful resolution to a bad situation. Sev agreed that it was probably better to pay them off this way.

'Tell all the workers I will pay them the money they give to these bandits back, so each of our workers will get the $20 a month back from me.' He said that the workers would be very grateful for this solution but we still had to sort out their demands for a $50 payment for each RTX bike that we make in the factory and $75 for each new model. Sash had already arranged a meeting with them at the Planeta Hotel at eleven in the morning, so after four hours sleep on Sev's settee I was woken by Irina to say breakfast was now nearly ready, so if I wanted to have a wash and brush up first it would be 10 minutes.

All cleaned up I sat and had breakfast with all the family, Tom, Sev's youngest son, asked me in pidgin English if I had brought him the toy Jaguar I had promised him on my last visit to Sev's apartment.

'No Tom, I didn't forget you.' Opening my briefcase I took out a die cast model of a Jaguar Mark 2 in bright red, just as he had asked for. The look on his face was worth carrying it all the way to Belarus, and during the next 20 minutes, while me and Sev finished talking, Tom raced round and round the room with his new toy.

'OK lets go to the factory and tell the workers about the deal I am going to do with them, concerning topping up their wages every month.' At the factory we went round each worker and Sev told them all individually what I had told him to say, that the Mafia payments would cost them nothing, the money they paid out would be repaid to them at the end of each month. They were all very pleased about this private arrangement, but now it was time to go to the Planeta hotel to meet the new Gestapo of Motovelo.

Sev stayed at the factory, and I collected Sash on the way.

'How many of these bandits are we supposed to be meeting?' I asked him and he said that he thought there were four of them coming. I was quite shocked when they walked into the lobby. These were not the usual Mafia types I'd had the misfortune to meet in the past, who were just leather clad clones of the KGB. These four looked all set for a western business meeting in their flash Italian suits and designer shoes. A table was selected and everybody sat down. The conversation was started off by a guy of about 25 years old who called himself Aszam.

'Mr Mason, we are here to offer you our services, to help your business run more efficiently in Belarus.' It runs very well now thanks, without your help.' I said.

'But you could have problems with building your bikes here if you cannot get the parts made.'

'Stop wasting my time.' I told him, 'and come to the point. What you are really wanting to do is blackmail me into paying you protection money.'

'Yes, of course, that is correct.' he answered. 'But what we offer you is protection, to make sure your operation here does not have any problems.'

'So you expect me to pay Motovelo for the bikes I have built there, and then pay you an extra $50 on each bike? Sorry but that is a stupid demand from your side, it is too much per bike.'

'What is your offer to us for the RTX model you make now?'

'$20 a bike, no more.' They talked amongst themselves for several minutes then Aszam came back with,

'How about $25 a bike?'

'No.' I answered. 'That's too much, lets settle on

$20 per bike for the model we now make and $30 per bike on any new models we make in the future.' In the end they all accepted these prices.

'How will you pay us?' was the next question that popped up.

'Every time a container is shipped to us in the UK, you will be paid by Sash in cash. We load 50 bikes into a 20 foot container and 100 bikes in a 40 foot container, so it's easy to calculate how much we will have to pay you'

'Sash tells us that you carry a Russian Government emergency button.'

'You mean this?' I said to Aszam producing the small black box out of my brief case.

'How long have you had one of these black boxes, Mr Mason?'

'Nearly 20 years.' I answered him.

'Have you ever used it?'

'Yes, on two occasions, and both times the protectors arrived and sorted the problem out for me.'

The meeting was now finished. With no more to say me and Sash stood up said our goodbyes to the blackmailing bas...ds, then went back to Sash's apartment for lunch. Over the meal we discussed the meeting about the new type and style of Russian Mafia and we both agreed the meeting went better than we expected.

'The box really impressed them all.' Sash said. Aszam had told the others never to physically touch anybody who carried one of these black boxes or it would cause very much trouble for them.

Now I was back at Motovelo, Sev told me he was being fired as Motovelo's chief designer at the end of the week. He looked a bit put out when I told him.

'That's good, it's brilliant news, now it means you can work full time with our company in England.'

'But who will pay my salary now?' he asked.

'RTX will pay you now. How much was Motovelo paying you a week?' I asked him.

'$40 a week.'

'So RTX will pay you $60 a week, is that enough?' but I could see by his face that it was. He told Irina he had been sacked from the factory as their chief designer but I had offered him a job working for RTX full time, running our department inside the plant. I told him it may also involve doing some work in England and would this be a problem to them both.

'No its not a problem, I like going to England.'

'How about going to Kovrov?' I asked him. 'Just before I left England to come here I got a fax from them asking if we would be interested in helping them develop their bikes, as we've done with Motovelo over the years. How do you fancy having a trip to their factory to check out what bikes they have that may be of interest to us?'

'I would love to go and take a look at their plant and check out their bikes.' he said. 'I will ring them now and arrange a date for the visit.' Picking the phone up he rang Kovrov and within five minutes he was talking to the Director of the factory. He told him it was Sevolod Klenisky, the former chief designer for Motovelo, in Minsk, now the full time representative of RTX UK. He then arranged with the Director to visit him and his factory in two weeks time on our behalf.

Sev told me that when we were at the factory that morning he had heard a rumour that there was a possibility that Ustymchuck may leave Motovelo to go into politics in the Belarusian Government. This would mean that Yasvinsky, his deputy, could take over as the new Director of the factory and he thought that that may have been the real reason behind him being asked to leave his position. I wanted to know if this would affect our RTX dept but he assured me that it definitely wouldn't.

'The factory make good money from your RTX bike's manufacturing division, and so do the Mafia now, so they both have a vested interest in keeping it going.' I stayed at Sevs again that night as I had to catch the train back to Holland at 2 am.

I arrived back in England two days later and told John about the latest situation in Motovelo, and that Sev now worked for us full time as he had left the employment of Motovelo, and the fact that we now had to pay the Mafia $20 on each RTX we made. John was all for packing it in, as the Mafia was getting entrenched in the factory but we both agreed to give it another year to see how things panned out, but we decided not to put the three new RTX models we had developed into production, as the Mafia situation at Motovelo was only going to get worse not better.

The sales of our Champ and Traka Garelli engined kids/adult bikes was going from strength to strength and we were now averaging 400 a month, and the small 50cc quad John had worked on at Monto in India was proving to be a sales winner as well, averaging 100 month. The Monto factory in India never gave us any trouble at all in the eight years we worked with them, they did everything we ever asked of them and every six months we had visits to the UK from the owner, Chand Mehter and Dinesh Tandon his nephew and manager. This, along with the fact that John visited the factory in India every year to work on new models, provided a good solid partnership with very good profitable sales for us and for them, plus trouble free business for both sides, and all this was achieved without any Mafia problems what so ever. It genuinely was the most stress free factory we ever worked with in the World.

We introduced Lifan, the big Chinese factory we worked with in China, to Monto Motors. We arranged a meeting between them which resulted in them forming a joint partnership to import Lifan made, part assembled, bikes from China into India where the assembly was finished and the bikes sold on the Indian market by Monto Motors. We didn't make any money from setting up this deal between them, but it's nice to know that without our initial introduction it might not have happened.

I told John that Sev was going to visit the Kovrov plant the following week to see if they made any bikes that we could modify and improve. After that Sev would work in the RTX department for a week, to get the next shipment of RTX twin shocks ready, and to prepare the first and last batch of 20 new 212 Mono Disc Trials bikes, so they could be shipped in the container with the next batch of RTX twin shock Trials bikes. Now, due to the increased Mafia involvement and demands at the factory no more RTX 212 Mono Discs Trials bikes would be made at Motovelo, so if you've got one hang on to it, as it's going to become a collectors bike.

When Sev had them all loaded into the container for shipping he was coming over to England to work with us for one month, to learn how we operated our business here in the west compared to what he was used to in Belarus. Sev had telephoned from Kovrov saying he was quite pleased with the welcome he had received at the plant by the Director and staff. The factory was a lot bigger than he thought it was going to be. His visit had been a good one and he had taken many photos of bikes and engines which we could utilize.

Sev arrived in England the following week with some good photos of the bikes Kovrov were still making. Two of the bikes stood out. One was a 50cc, three speed, two stroke with a Derby engine, cantilever frame, and 16 inch wheels fitted, which, with modifications would make a great bike for kids aged ten to fifteen years old. The other bike I thought was of interest was a mono shocked, four speed, two stroke, reed valve 200cc full sized bike, plus they also made a three wheeled 200cc Trike that looked like it would convert to a quad, or parts from it could be used to make a quad.

I asked Sev to ring the Kovrov factory and order some samples, two of the 50cc bike and three of the 200cc bike, plus two 200cc trikes. The samples arrived within two weeks. One 50cc and one 200cc were taken out of their boxes and checked over and given a quick PDI before been taken out for a severe thrashing around the local quarry at South Ferriby. The bikes were hammered around all that afternoon and apart from adjusting the rear chains on both sample bikes, they took all we could throw at them that day, with no mechanical problems at all.

The 50cc was fitted with a copy of a Spanish Derby engine, now made under licence in Russia and this really was a cracking little engine. We sold many thousands of bikes fitted with this type of Russian copy, Derby engine, and over four years, genuinely, the warranty rate was unbelievable low. They just seemed to keep on going forever.

The Russian 200cc two stroke engine was also very strong and reliable, and again never gave us many problems, and with a few mods to the porting, on the sample bikes cylinder barrel and head, it was made to perform quite well. With all the mods, we got it up from 16hp to 20hp, then we asked the factory in Russia to incorporate all our modifications into the standard production 200cc engines. Both these bikes were put into our ever expanding Champ Range as the Champ 50cc Super cross and the Champ A 200cc Scrambler.

We managed to build two prototype quads by using many of the components from the trikes. A Farm Quad, FQ200cc and a Sports Quad, SQ200cc. We did this by modifying a standard A 200cc Scrambler solo bike, and using a lot of the components from the trike, such as the complete back axle and differential, and the large trike offroad wheels and tyres, and with some heavy duty off road buggy parts fitted, it completed the steering. I got the factory to airfreight six trike, 18 inch wheels and tyres, and another A200 solo bike across to us. The finished quads looked very good, and were very strong. They also had the advantage of having a reverse gear fitted. We spent nearly two weeks testing both models on Easington Beach, I lost count of the hours we spent up there riding them, but it was a good excuse for having a lot of fun on the deserted winter seaside beach.

The sports quad was christened the Champ SQ200cc Sand Quad and the farm quad the Champ FQ200cc Bigfoot. Both of the quads were fitted with massive 18 inch wide, deep grip, tubeless tyres front and rear. While we were testing them on the beach at Easington a local farmer, out walking his dog, took a great interest in the Bigfoot farm quad and asked if he could have a go on it. After putting his dog onto the rear carrier he drove off for about 5 minutes, then returned, grinning like a Cheshire cat.

'Are you here tomorrow testing?' he asked.

'Yes we'll be here for the rest of the week.' I told him.

'Then put me down for one.' he said. 'It's great to ride and will be ideal for my farm.' The next day he turned up with a deposit of £100 in cash for a Champ

FQ200cc Bigfoot farm quad.

'Let me know when the first quads arrive. That's my farm over there.' he said pointing to a large farm set back from the cliff top.

While we were at the beach testing a thought occurred to me. Would the standard A200cc, solo bike also convert to a two wheeled 'quad'? Was it possible to modify this bike to take the quads 14 inch wide wheels and tyres? John and Wayne continued the quad testing on the beach while I stayed in our workshop to convert a standard A200cc solo to the big wide quad wheels.

I made a set of wide front fork yokes to take the wide front wheel and then made a special wide, box section swinging arm, with the drive shaft taken through the front of it just behind the swinging arm pivot bolt. With the two spare trike wheels and tyres fitted into place the first prototype Champ SB200cc, 'Sand Bike' as I called it, was complete. The tyres were so wide the bike stood upright on its own, with out needing a stand to hold it there. In the weeks testing that followed it was amazing just how it performed in deep mud and soft sand, it was just about unstoppable. It was also apparent it would be brilliant in the snow.

Top: Original prototype Sand bike I developed
Bottom: Original prototype Farm quad I developed

Champ SX60 we developed for Kovrov Plant

Now the prototype quads and bikes were finished, I invited the Kovrov factory's Director, and his sales manager, to visit us in the UK to see what they thought to the finished prototypes. When they arrived they were able to see just what we had developed, in the last month, from their standard production bikes and the standard trike. They were gob smacked to say the least. They were absolutely amazed at how we had developed two totally different quads from their standard 200cc solo bike and parts taken from their trike. Also the conversion John had done on the 50cc, Derby engined bike, was also an eye opener for them. It now looked right up to date with the latest moto cross styling, based on Yamaha YZ125 MX plastics and a new, totally redesigned, graphics set he'd made to fit the Yamaha plastics. It now looked a totally modern bike, fitted with the new plastics and graphics, as well as a new seat, new power flow overhead exhaust system, and Dunlop MX tyres, plus, a bigger Jikov carburettor had been fitted to provide more power.

They were so impressed with what we had done that they agreed to signing an exclusive, five year, worldwide contract with us, with an option of a further five years if we wanted. They signed this agreement before they returned home to Russia and this gave us the sole selling and distribution rights for all the new model bikes and quads we had created. The contract was for the entire world apart from Russia and Iran.

The first order was for 200 of the 50cc Derby engined bikes, without plastics, seats, or exhaust pipes fitted. We would fit the new, modified parts onto the bikes in England. We also ordered 200, A200cc solos without tyres or plastics fitted. Again, the MX tyres and plastics would be fitted to them here in England. The prototype sports and farm quads developed here, were shipped back to the factory in Russia, to be copied and put onto the production line at the factory for us, and I placed an initial order with them for 150, SQ200cc sports quads and 150, FQ200cc farm quads. The AQ200cc, Sand Bike I had conceived, with the fat tyres, was also sent over to the factory for them to copy and put into full production. I ordered 200, AQ200cc Sand Bikes. Sev agreed to go to the Kovrov factory to oversee the work that would be involved in getting them all ready for production, and was very busy working at the factory on this new project for just over two months.

This was the year we found Squeak, a baby

pigeon, she was sat at the road side. She can't fly, can't feed herself, and is blind in one eye, as her mother had unwittingly fed her poisoned corn. She is part of our family, and we have looked after her for over twelve years now and have hand fed her, in the morning and at tea time, every day of that time.

One of the many things I discovered early on while working with the Russian motorcycle factories was, left to themselves, not a lot got improved on their bikes, as they were so busy working flat out to supply their own Russian home market with machines. Well I suppose if you're selling all the bikes you're making into your own country and your factories are working flat out, seven days a week just to try and keep up with demand, there is no incentive to improve the bikes. What I managed to do was convince them that sooner or later they would fill up their home market and would then have to sell their bikes on the world markets, so improvements on the bikes needed to start to be done NOW. As trained engineers they really were quite brilliant, and good people to work with, after all they had got their men to the moon and back again. British engineering never came near to achieving anything like that.

ROAD RACE KIDS

SET IN THE 1960'S THE FOUR HICKMAN KIDS HAVE THEIR
OWN PRACTICE TRACK ON THE FAMILY'S MUSHROOM FARM
WHICH IS LOCATED ON AN OLD WORLD WAR TWO AIRFIELD
IN NORTHERN LINCOLNSHIRE. TWO OF THE LADS, SIMON
14 AND NORMAN 13, ARE INTO SOLO BIKES AND THE TWO
YOUNGEST, JEFF 9 AND LINDA 10, ARE INTO SIDECAR
RACING AND RIDE A SPECIALLY BUILT SIDECAR OUTFIT
MADE JUST FOR KIDS.

THIS BOOK FOLLOWS THE FOUR KIDS AS
THEY GROW UP AND DEVELOP THEIR OWN
RIDING AND RACING SKILLS AROUND
THEIR OWN TRACK.

Nev Mason

Chapter 24

One of the major problems we found, while working with the Chinese, was as soon as a factory had a fully developed motorcycle ready to put on the market everybody else in that area copied it. There was no loyalty amongst the component suppliers, they would sell to anybody who would buy parts from them. In the nine years we worked with the Chinese this was always a continuing problem. As soon as we put a new model out on the market a copy appeared within a very short space of time. This did not bode well for long term business, or for market stability. We persevered with them for nine years but by then the factories were so desperate they were selling bikes to anybody who would buy from them.

A local fish and chip shop owner in Immingham brought in a container of Chinese bikes and sold them on the UK market without any spares, or sales back up, resulting in a lot of dissatisfied customers and many broken down bikes around the Immingham area. He then, conveniently, just disappeared.

China was now fast becoming a country we did

not particularly like dealing with anymore. At least in India and Russia the factories were relatively stable, (apart from the Mafia). They didn't stab each other in the back just to get sales, as now seemed to be the normal way of doing business in China.

Around this time though, we did start to get more trouble with the new Mafia idiots at Motovelo. They wanted to put the price we paid them, to keep our RTX project going inside the factory, up from $20 per bike to $60 per bike, starting at the end of the month. I rang Sash and told him to go to the factory to find out when the next shipment of RTX Trials bikes would be completed and ready for loading into their shipping containers. He rang me back later that night.

'There will be 200 RTX Trials bikes ready to load into two 40 foot containers in three days time and they will go to the port at St. Petersburg the day after that.' he said, 'then, they should be in England three days later.' Quickly I worked the time scale out, that would give us another sixteen days before the Mafia intended to increase their new exorbitant blackmailing price to us. Me and John had already made a decision, six months previously, that the moment the Mafia upped their protection demands we would stop the

RTX project at Motovelo.

As soon as the two containers of bikes arrived at our depot in England from Belarus I sent a fax to the Director at the Motovelo factory telling him that unfortunately, due to the new, stupid demands from the Mafia in Minsk, we were stopping, with immediate effect, all the RTX production at his factory. Because of the Mafia's increased demands the project was no longer viable. Within a few days we had a reply from Director Yazvinski, saying that he now had the problem fully under control at the factory and could we go to Belarus to discuss the cooperation between us, and continue the RTX project at the plant.

The RTX trials bike was our original concept, and as such we owned the world wide Intellectual Property Rights to it. Because the design of the RTX bike was ours, we could build and sell it anywhere we wanted in the world. Just where it was built was up to us. My very good friend in the Ukraine, Anatoli Miychenco, my old Neval Motorcycles technician, checked out the true situation at the Motovelo factory for me regarding the Mafia. He spent a full day in the factory before confirming that there was no future working with them anymore. His reply was that we had made the right decision to pull out of working with Motovelo. The new Mafia, he said, were now firmly entrenched throughout the factory, and they are far too strong, even for Director Yazvinski to try and move them out.

After 24 years of dealing with Motovelo in Belarus, we finally and sadly closed the doors on working with them ever again. We would concentrate on selling the two hundred and thirty four RTX Trials bikes we had left in stock, and we had a good stock of spare parts, which we had built up over the years, to back up the remaining bikes.

We now decided to develop a new model RTX 125cc, 200cc and 250 cc four stroke Trials bikes. A twin shock, drum braked model, and a mono shock, disc braked model. This we achieved by making and developing two prototypes over the next two years, but they were never to go into production. You will find out later in my story why they did not make it.

The two sample offroad buggies had finally arrived so we took them up to our airfield at Elsham to try them out and we enjoyed a full afternoon driving them round our test track. The buggy fitted with the Planeta 350cc engine was quite fast, but the vibration

RTX TTL200

NEW FOR 2004

UK RECOMMENDED RETAIL PRICES FROM JUST £1495 inc VAT, Plus delivery charge

A NEW RANGE OF FOUR STROKE ENTRY LEVEL TRIALS MOTORCYCLES DESIGNED AND ASSEMBLED IN THE UK, BY OFFROAD LEISURE UK, TEL 0044 (1652) 660375, MANUFACTURERS OF CHAMP, TRAKA, DIRTBIKE AND RTX M/CYCLES

New RTX 4 stroke Trials bike, never put into production because we retired

389

Some of the many successes of RTX Trials bikes

this engine caused was very bad, in fact it was terrible. The other buggy had a 125 cc Minsk engine fitted, and the problem with this one was the buggy's weight which was too heavy for the 125cc motor to push around. We concluded that the buggies were good, but the engines were not suitable for them. Back in the workshop we took out the Planeta engine and fitted in its place, a new Honda 270cc, industrial four stroke engine, with auto clutch. Now all the vibration had totally gone. It was very quiet, had a reasonable turn of speed with quite good acceleration, and it gave about 45 mph top speed, which was enough. Now it was real fun to drive. We then thrashed this buggy around for a week at the airfield without any problems. We decided to stick to this one model, fitted with the Honda 270cc engine.

Sev rang the buggy factory for me and ordered 200 buggies, without engines, one hundred to be in red and one hundred in blue. Honda were then telephoned and 200, 270cc engines with auto clutch fitted were ordered for delivery to us in eight weeks time, which would coincide with the first buggy delivery from Mogilev arriving.

In the meantime we had a meeting with British

Aero Space to find out if they had any interest in working with the aircraft factory in the Ukraine that had shown me the special thin, strong, alloy in Minsk. They were given the sample piece of alloy to examine, and just sat looking at it in disbelief. It was very obvious they had not seen anything like it before. I told both of the Directors at the meeting the story I had been told and asked if they wanted the full contact information of the Ukrainian factory so they could contact them direct. The sample was left with them, along with the name of the aircraft plant and who to contact there. About a year later I received a very nice letter from the Director of the aircraft factory in the Ukraine, thanking me for helping them to work with British Aero Space with the lightweight, thin alloy sheet. I never ever got any thanks at all or even any acknowledgment from the British factory, just a simple thank you letter from them would have been nice, but not to worry, life goes on.

In 1998, me and Val visited Anatol and his family in Kiev. Anatol had visited us in England in 1997 and asked me to go across to the Dnieper factory to try and help get it back on its feet. We spent an enjoyable two days at his home with his wife Neala and his now grown up kids. I was amazed to see he was still running the Ford Fairlane Estate car me and Alan had bought him all those years ago and it looked in far better condition than when we originally bought it for him.

On day three Anatol drove us to the Dnieper plant in Kiev. What a change 10 years had made. On my last visit to the factory in 1980 it was a hive of activity and expansion, now it was like a ghost factory. Before, many thousands of workers were working twenty four hours a day turning out 650cc MT10 36 sidecar outfits and solos, but now all the assembly lines were empty. Knowing what it was like before, on our last visit and seeing it now as it lay totally silent was really heart wrenching. Introduced to the new director, Mr Mazurenko, who told us the production was down to just thirty bikes a week.

'What do you think is the best thing for me to do, apart from committing suicide?' he joked. (I hoped he was joking).

'There is only one way to go.' I told him, 'downsize your operation and sell off or rent out all the parts of the plant you no longer need.'

'We have already started to do this,' he

explained, 'so far we have sold off about 30% of the buildings we no longer use. We also have a large transport company interested in renting the main, massive production building, for storage use, which would leave us with about one hectare of buildings for our own manufacturing use. Would you be interested in helping us make our bikes more acceptable for the West , as you did before, and show us what is required to make them better to sell?'

'Do you still have your old MT12 750cc side valve engine casting moulds and gearbox moulds to enable you to recast and manufacture this engine?' Anatol was very quick to point out that they had scrapped it all only last year, which I thought was a shame as the 750cc side valve engine would have made a good motor for a retro chopper.

'OK,' I said 'airfreight me a standard 650cc Dnieper solo across and I will see what I can make from it.' We spent two days at the factory seeing what parts were still available for use and before we left the factory I signed a letter of cooperation and a full letter of intent with Mazurenko and the factory for ten years.

A friend of Anatol wanted a meeting with me before we returned to England so me, Val and Anatol met him over lunch. He turned out to be the son of Ivan, the guy me and Alan had met many years earlier, who had told us he didn't want to work with our English company, and who Anatol had got his red book out to that day, but as time had passed, Ivan the Terrible, as I called him had become a big help to us. He thought the name I gave him was very amusing and he had helped us by making sure all our UK bikes were fitted with the correct red star military quality components.

Then Ivan junior totally surprised me. He knew that we had been working with the Chinese factories, developing bikes with Lifan and Zongshen because he had a friend who worked at Lifan who had told him about us. I looked across at Anatol.

'Did you know about this?' I asked him.

'Yes Nev I did.' he said with a big grin on his face. 'Ivan junior wants to ask you if you will help him buy and import Chinese motorcycles into the Ukraine. I'll work with him, to help set up a dealer sales network in the Ukraine.' Talk about Coals to Newcastle now it looks like I'm getting involved in importing Chinese motorcycles into Russia. Anyway, I agreed to help them.

We spent the next day with Anatol in his Ford Fairlane Estate car being chauffeured around, doing a full tour of all the Kiev sights, and there are some good ones. The next day it was back on the plane and I was glad to see it was American made, and soon we were back home again.

It took about five weeks for the standard Dnieper Solo to arrive in the UK. When it did arrive I stripped it all down and cut the frame in half at the back of the gearbox, just keeping the front frame diamond, then dropped the engine down at the front by two inches and put the front mounting bracket below the frame tube. This kept the engine level, but meant the frame could now be laid back to rake out the front fork angle. I made up a set of 25mm parallel tube front forks then fitted a 21 inch front wheel with a ribbed tyre and a pair of 14 inch pull back bars. I made up two types of rear ends, one was rigid and one was sprung, with 40% angle laid down shocks. A single carb was also fitted to make the engine more flexible, and a single seat finished it off.

Built up it was taken to our airfield for testing and because it was now so light, it performed very well. It also handled and steered a lot better than I had

Top: The prototype chopper I designed
for the Dnieper Factory

Meeting with directors at Dnieper Factory

expected it to and everybody who saw this bike thought it looked better with the rigid back end format. My calculations were that this bike could have been produced at a very low cost and also put in production very quickly. I know it would have been a top seller for the factory worldwide, and the Dnieper plant was very keen to make it but sadly, they went bust before they could put the bike in production . It was a pity, I was going to give them an order for 250 of them to start them off.

They did come back to me a year later, to see about producing it again after they had managed to get refinanced, but it was too late then as I had already scrapped the original prototype bike I had made, which had been christened by me as the B52 RC. I had also planned a new more modern up to date disc braked 750cc Military outfit .

Lifan was not interested in selling any fewer than 500 bikes at a time, so I got Ivan junior's bikes through Changming a much smaller company than Lifan. I knew their quality was good as I'd had some bikes from them in the past. Ivan ordered 250, 50cc four speed four stroke road bikes from me, and I then organised the delivery for him to Kiev. He got the first delivery of bikes within eight weeks and his sales of these went very well, so he ordered another batch of 250 bikes.

A few months after this I got a phone call from Anatols wife Neala. Anatol had died from a heart attack. He had run out of his normal heart tablets so he had bought some on the black market from a Mafia supplier and they turned out to be made from compressed flour. This was another very bad day in my life as Anatol had become a true, valued friend. I sent $1000 to Neala, to pay for his funeral, as she and her family could not afford to pay for it.

After the next delivery of bikes I put Ivan junior in contact with the Changming factory so he could get his bikes direct from them in the future. My heart was no longer in this project, Anatol had gone and so, unfortunately, had my interest.

NEV HAS DONE MORE FOR OUR MOTORCYCLE FACTORIES IN RUSSIA THAN ANYBODY ELSE I KNOW FROM THE WESTERN WORLD. HE SHOWED US HOW WE COULD MAKE MANY IMPROVEMENTS TO OUR MOTORBIKES. BECAUSE OF HIS HELP WE NOW SELL THEM MUCH BETTER IN THE WORLD.
QUOTE FROM-ANATOL MIYCHENKO-RUSSIA.

Chapter 25

For the next 4 years we concentrated on continually expanding the business and increasing our range of bikes and products that were now being sold worldwide, but eventually the work load started to become too much for us all. We had a family meeting at the end of 2004 and decided to cut down on our many worldwide commitments.

The first to go was the music business, as this took up a lot of my time and was very expensive to maintain, so our record company was moved on to a Russian company in Moscow. The replacement Honda MX radiators section of the business was moved on to a friend in Canada and all the Chinese factories we dealt with were sent letters informing them we no longer wished to continue business with them due to their double dealing business methods, and that we felt they were no longer trustworthy to deal with. This got rid of the four factories in China we had worked with for over nine years but it also, unfortunately, meant terminating the new model RTX 125cc, 200cc and 250cc four stroke Trials bike project, which had been due to be built at one of these, now terminated, factories in China. Fortunately they never got their hands on the prototype RTX Trials bikes so were unable to copy them.

The next year proved that the right decision had been made by us all at that meeting, as my health went down to an all time low. It got so bad at times, I could only work for a couple of hours a day (heart and diabetics). John's health was also not good and he was having to cope with my lack of involvement in running the business, so his work load and stress levels were very high.

Now it was 2005 and decision time. We had plenty of money in the bank, and all our tax was fully paid up to date. We still had plenty of assets left to sell, and didn't owe our suppliers any money, they were all paid up to date. We could all retire if we chose to, so the united family decision to retire was made and then implemented.

We notified all the remaining factories we still worked with about the health situation of me and John, and of our intention to retire from business. We shared out the remaining stock of bikes and parts we had left between our distributors. Some stock we sold to them, but a lot of stock was given to them, free of charge, as

Our family of dogs in our back field

LARGE FARM HOUSE, LAND AND BUILDINGS IN MANCHE, NORMANDY IDEAL FOR EQUESTRIAN USE OR GITES

LARGE TRADITIONAL STONE AND BRICK FARMHOUSE IN A COURTYARD WITH IMPRESSIVE STONE ARCHED ENTRANCE. APPROX 12.5 ACRES (5 HECTARES) OF GRASSLAND (POSSIBILITY OF APPROX 6 ACRES EXTRA LAND IF REQUIRED), TWO PONDS, NUMEROUS OUTBUILDINGS IN GOOD CONDITION AND EXTRA SELF CONTAINED ACCOMMODATION, ALL DOWN A PRIVATE LANE ON THE EDGE OF A VILLAGE 2 MILES FROM CARENTAN, MANCHE, NORMANDY.

THE HOUSE CONSISTS OF A THREE STOREY CENTRAL SECTION WITH TWO, TWO STOREY WINGS AT EACH END. ONE WING HAS BEEN CONVERTED INTO SELF CONTAINED ACCOMMODATION. THE FULL HOUSE HAS BEEN UPVC DOUBLE GLAZED IN THE ORIGINAL STYLE AND NEW OIL FUELLED CENTRAL HEATING SYSTEM FITTED.

SELF CONTAINED ACCOMMODATION
A LARGE OPEN PLAN LIVING ROOM, DINING AREA AND FULLY EQUIPPED FITTED HYGENA KITCHEN WITH A BEDROOM AND EN-SUITE SHOWER ROOM. THIS AREA IS FULLY REFURBISHED WITH THE WALLS, CEILINGS AND TILED FLOOR HAVING ALL BEEN FULLY INSULATED.

MAIN HOUSE - GROUND FLOOR
LARGE, WELL PROPOERTIONED LIVING ROOM WITH GRANITE FIREPLACE, LARGE KITCHEN (USABLE BUT NEEDS FITTING OUT), TWO UTILITY ROOMS, ONE HOUSING THE NEW OIL FUELLED CENTRAL HEATING BOILER, BATHROOM WITH BATH, SHOWER, TWIN HANDBASINS AND SEPARATE TOILET. A VARNISHED WOOD STAIRCASE GOES ALL THE WAY TO THE TOP FLOOR AND THE STAIRWELL IS PAINTED IN A NEUTRAL COLOUR.

MIDDLE FLOOR
THREE BEDROOMS (ALL REQUIRING DECORATION) WITH MARBLE FIREPLACES, ONE WITH PIPEWORK INSTALLED FOR A BATHROOM, LANDING AND STORAGE SPACE.

TOP FLOOR
TOTALLY REFURBISHED WITH NEW VELUX WINDOWS, LARGE LANDING, THREE BEDROOMS, TOILET AND SHOWER ROOM, ALL NEWLY FITTED AND DECORATED WITH SOME EXPOSED BEAMS AND HARDWOOD FLOOR.

OUTSIDE
THERE ARE LARGE, TWO STOREY OUTBUILDINGS/BARNS ON TWO SIDES OF THE COURTYARD WHICH WERE REBUILT IN THE 50's AND ARE IN GOOD CONDITION WITH BEAUTIFUL ROOF BEAMS AND BEAM AND BLOCK FLOORS. WOULD EASILY CONVERT TO GITES OR STABLES, PLUS SINGLE STOREY OPEN BUILDINGS ON THE REMAINING SIDE. THERE ARE TWO WILD LIFE FISH PONDS FLANKING THE LANE.
THE FULL HOUSE ROOF HAS BEEN FITTED WITH NEW STAINLESS STEEL CLIPS, THE CHIMNEYS HAVE BEEN REPOINTED AND NEW GUTTERING AND FLASHINGS FITTED. ALL INTERNAL WOODWORK TREATED.

The big farm, land and buildings I bought in Normandy, France

a goodwill gesture, and to cover any future warranty work they may have to undertake on the bikes they had already sold. We then dismantled the remaining business, and put our large hillside house on the market and went to France in search of our new home, and new life. Our South Ferriby house sold in four months, so I bought a large twenty acre, former farm, complete with three large barns and a big fourteen roomed house.

It was not far from the World War II, D Day landing beaches, and John bought a smaller, eight bed roomed house with 4 acres, nearby.

After all my years of working 100% flat out in everything I did, trying to achieve the goals which I set myself, this new slow pace of life took me many months to adjust to. All my efforts now went into getting the farmhouse upgraded and modernised. It was fitted with new double glazed windows, 36 of them, plus new central heating, and new fitted kitchen and bathrooms. All the gardens, court yard and orchard were kicked into shape with a mini digger, and a new Honda 25 hp, ride on lawnmower, was bought for mowing the orchard and the 3 acres of lawns that surrounded the house. Driving this around cutting the grass on a nice sunny day was very therapeutic and relaxing and I found myself making excuses to go outside and cut the lawn. It was also very useful for driving round the farm on, taking Sam our English Labrador dog for a walk.

Deborah our daughter also moved across to live here in the farm with her partner Dave and four sons Matt, Dan ,Tom and Jake. My health vastly improved due to the more laid back, slower pace, and way of life living in France, plus my heart and diabetic treatment was also much better, due to our local French doctor's thorough investigations into my problems. He changed over 40% of my previously prescribed, medication to a different type, and suddenly I felt 20 years younger.

Life was great for another six months kicking our new home into shape until Deb and Dave dropped the bombshell that they were returning back to the UK because Deb and the older kids had not settled. They missed their friends and it was very difficult for the boys, learning to speak French at school. Anyway, Deb and family moved back to England which left a big hole in our lives. This void was partly filled when Val's sister Christine and her husband Eddie bought a small cottage in the country, not too far from us, which they

The prototype CNC cut alloy BMX bikes I developed

The Gatecrasher bike developed from my original design

set about extending to accommodate Greta, Val and Christine's mother. Greta stayed with us at the farm for a short time while work was in progress on the cottage extension.

Having got the farm renovated I started playing around with a new type of push bike frame design. I built up a prototype frame for a mountain jump bike and asked some French lads to test it out at the local BMX track. They all seemed to like it and spent many hours thrashing it about. As I was now retired, I didn't want to get involved in making or selling this new bike so I contacted Falcon Cycles at Brigg to see if they had any interest in its manufacture and sales. It turned out they were interested, so I did a deal with them, and we jointly registered the frame design in both my and their names, and I now get a royalty payment from Falcon for every bike that they make. The only thing I didn't particularly like was the bright fluorescent green colour Falcon chose to paint the frame, but somebody must like the colour because it's selling all over the UK even Asda Amazon and Argos are retailing it.

Now, just to keep my mind occupied, I set about designing a full sized armour suit for display purposes. I sent a friend of mine, Yuri in Latvia, a sketch of what

I wanted and the full measurements of the size I wanted it to be. I had known this guy for many years, he was one of the old school, who could hand make anything in metal. Now 78 years old, he had spent a lifetime hand crafting motorcycle and car parts. He completed the first steel prototype armour suit in two months. Standing just over 6 feet high it was most impressive.

I asked him if it was possible for him to make it in 16 gauge brass and he said it would be no problem and three months later a DHL van turned up at the farm with two boxes. Unpacking them both revealed a fantastic dress armour suit, in gleaming 16 gauge brass plate. When it was all fully assembled it really was a mind blowing piece of craftsmanship. They were very expensive to make. Yuri had calculated about two months for each complete, hand crafted, brass armour suit to be made, and the cost would be $2000 each, for the brass suits, and $2500 for the suits in 16 gauge copper.

Just seeing the photos of the first prototype brass armour suite Yuri had produced for me, brought in an order from a friend in Scotland, for 10 complete armour suit sets, 5 to be in 16 gauge brass and 5 in 16 gauge copper. My mark up was to be $250 on each suit but unfortunately, halfway through the first order, Yuri fell ill and died a month later. His skills have not been possible to replace, as he worked alone, so I stopped the project and now in my living room I have the two original prototypes he made for me. They really are superb, six foot high tributes to his craftsmanship, one suit is in steel and one is in brass.

My friend in Scotland got the five suits Yuri had finished, three in brass and two in copper. The money that was left owing to Yuri for the five production suits he had finished, was sent to his wife in Latvia. He had already been paid by me for the two original steel and brass prototype suits.

Three years drifted past, living at the slowed down pace of life in France. John had recently sold his house, so when he received an invitation from Colin Hill, one of our old UK bike distributors, to stay at his holiday home in southern France in the Pyrenees, John and his family spent five days there. On returning home he announced that he would like to move there to live in this beautiful mountain terrain. Two weeks later me, Val, and Johns family went to look at the area and within a day John had put a bid in, on a large transport complex with a bungalow attached to it, all sat alongside a fast flowing mountain river, and just a week after we returned back, his offer on the property was accepted.

'NOW WHAT' was the question I asked him.

'Well it looks like we may be moving again.' was his answer. Within two months John's house sale was completed and he and his family had moved and were living at their new residence in the south of France

Me and Val were now sat on our own, in a very large fourteen roomed farmhouse which was too big for most people, So plan B was hatched. I would sell off the farmhouse and the surrounding lawns including the orchard, and keep the large barns and ponds and sixteen acres of land, in case we ever wanted to move back there in the future, so before we left, we obtained planning permission to convert the barns to residential use. It took just over five months to sell the farmhouse, lawns and orchard before me and Val also moved down to Johns new house

We had a new riverside apartment built for us at the side of Johns complex and I must admit the weather in the south is a lot better, and so is the scenery, with its huge mountain ranges and lots of very old castles and historic hillside villages to investigate. I have kept

Val's Mum's 80th birthday

Debbie's boys playing on small bikes I designed

myself occupied and busy by designing and building a totally new type of CNC, BMX alloy bike frame, plus a CNC alloy framed ski bike, and you never know, some day they may get put into production.

Many of the people I dealt with worldwide, over my lifetime, still keep in contact with me, but now I have no day to day business interests to attend to. Val and I now content ourselves in life with the adventure of driving around the many hundreds of miles of forest roads, going up and down and around, in the Pyrenees Mountains, exploring in our Land Rover. So far we have seen and photographed lots of wild boar, many different types of deer, and we have even seen wolves, eagles and pine martens. There are hundreds of enduro bikes out every weekend in the summer using the forest trails, most of them are Honda, KTM and TM and it's good to sit at the side of the forest tracks in the Land Rover and watch them go by. It brings back good memories of the many years of off road, bike riding I was lucky enough to enjoy. I am still designing special parts for bikes, plus now I also keep 22 pigeons as pets in a new loft I had built for them. I never ever saw myself, in my past way of life, keeping pigeons as a hobby but life slows you down and changes your views. I have gone from a lifetime working flat out at 100% in everything I did, to a nice, slow pace, for the life that I and Val now live only 60% effort is required. In late 2010 my brother Pete sadly died in England of a heart attack, yet another chapter of my life gone.

Motorcycles, racing them, designing them, developing them, plus dealing and working with all those factories worldwide. I never ever considered what I did as work, it was just a great exciting way of life, to create an empire working on something I loved doing surrounded by a very good loving family.

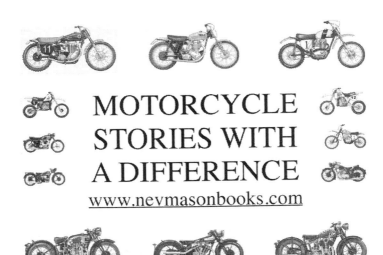

MOTORCYCLE
STORIES WITH
A DIFFERENCE
www.nevmasonbooks.com

Complete Regent Honda CX Outfits
we designed and sold

They say life begins at 40

Top: Me and Sam (Hell - that's another 30 years gone by!)
Bottom: Val & Pesky the pigeon at our new riverside apartment

Sam insisted on showing you his pink pig.